Dispatches from the Rust Belt

The Best of Belt Magazine

First Printing, 2014

ISBN-13: 978-0-9859441-7-9

Belt Publishing
1667 E. 40th Street #1G1
Cleveland, Ohio 44120
http://www.beltmag.com

Book design by Haley Stone
Cover design by Haley Stone

Table of Contents

IV. Cities

V. Politics

VI. First Person

Contributors

Introduction

Anne Trubek

When *Belt Magazine launched one year ago,* we did so for one basic reason: We felt that Cleveland and other cities in the Rust Belt were being defined by outside media that didn't know us. We wanted to tell our own story ourselves.

So we assembled writers, engaged citizens, academic experts, history buffs, and all sorts of people who live and work here to write about who we are. Some of our stories are long-form investigative journalism, some are essays about the arts and historic preservation, and many are thoughtful commentaries about economic issues. Quite frankly, we are proud of how we have progressed in the past year by engaging people who are interested in issues that matter. Our numbers bear this out: visits to our site continue to increase and the number of people who have supported us by buying memberships keeps growing. People join Belt to be part of a community and to acknowledge our commitment to pay writers, to edit carefully, and to have an independent voice.

We believe strongly in our business model. We want our readers to feel that they are a part of what we publish. In return, we feel a connection with them that is personal, meaningful, and sustaining. Our readers are not anonymous analytics or numbers.

This anthology comprises the best pieces from Belt's first year: there is work from experienced journalists who recognized early on the importance of what we were doing—Laura Putre's graceful, literary coverage of politics and the arts, Dan McGraw's vital investigative pieces, Ted McClelland's in-depth feature on Buffalo's waterfront and Gordon Young on urban homesteading. There are also pieces from newer writers who found a voice with us—Amanda Shaffer's "Busing: A White Girl's Tale" received national recognition.

We started out heavily Cleveland-centric and expanded into the further reaches of the Rust Belt as the year went on—we'll continue to tell more and more stories from across the Rust Belt, with a special love for Cleveland since that's where we're based.

We look forward to the coming year of more stories, investigations, interviews, and essays—to critically examine the Rust Belt region of the United States, a place deserving of our honor, our criticism, and our undivided attention.

Anne Trubek
September 12, 2014

Dispatches from the Rust Belt

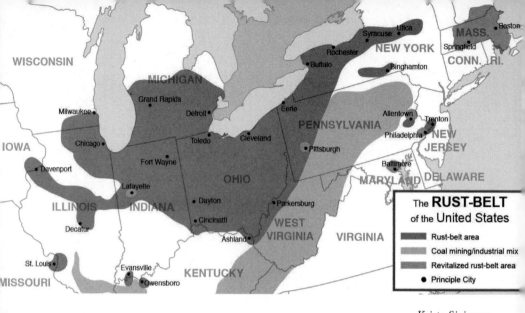

Krista Siniscarco

I. Where is the Rust Belt?

Belt Editors

I *t can be fun to debate* the borders of the post-industrial Midwest. Does Cincinnati count? What about Chicago? Or Columbus, which never had a large manufacturing base? Can Canada be part of the Rust Belt, as some geographers claim, or is it strictly an American phenomenon, a term coined by failed presidential candidate Walter Mondale during the 1984 election?

There is no one definitive answer, but we like this map, because it's well-reasoned and specific. It has the region extending east to the historically textile manufacturing cities of Massachusetts; west to Davenport (farm machinery), north to upstate New York and Milwaukee, and south to Kentucky.

Other maps have the Rust Belt extending as far north as Sheboygan and Green Bay, and others include Hamilton, Ontario.

But even consensus, true-blue Rust Belt cities aren't all alike. Though they share industry and a large Eastern European immigrant population, one area where they diverge is education. Writes Daniel Hartley, a research economist for the Cleveland Federal Reserve, "Cleveland and Detroit had the lowest proportion of residents over the age of 25 with a college degree or higher in 1970 (4 percent and 6 percent respectively). Thirty-six years later, the percentages had only inched up to 12 percent, but in Buffalo and Pittsburgh they had jumped to 20 and 31 percent respectively."

For editorial purposes at Belt, we'll loosely define the Rust Belt as any city in the northern Midwest that was built on late 19th/early 20th century manufacturing. Chicago's economy has always been too diverse to fit that description, but some areas of the South Side and surrounding suburbs qualify as Rust Belt. Columbus is peripherally Rust Belt, though its manufacturing base is the least of the Rust Belt cities. Wrote geographer Jim Russell in his Burgh Diaspora blog: "Among its Midwestern cohort, Columbus has the smallest industrial legacy. In 1970, it was the best-educated. If anything, the city has underplayed its advantages."

Belt will continue to map the Rust Belt geographically, historically, culturally and economically.

II. Arts and Culture

Dispatches from the Rust Belt

Mark Winegardner and the Rust Belt Dilemma

Erick Trickey

T*welve years ago,* Mark Winegardner confronted the Midwestern writer's dilemma. From Mark Twain to Ernest Hemingway to Toni Morrison, more great American writers have come from the Midwest than any other part of the country. Yet if we don't leave for "New York or someplace equally foreign," but try to create work based on our lives here, we risk being stuffed into a belittling pigeonhole: *regional writer.*

Winegardner's 2002 essay, "Toward a Literature of the Midwest," grew from the challenges he faced after writing Crooked River Burning, an epic historical novel set in Cleveland. In the piece (also published as "Writing Our Wrongs" in *Cleveland Magazine*), he recalled his fury when his publisher's marketing director called his novel a "strong regional book." He considered that a curse, a consignment to obscurity. An Ohioan who relocated to Florida, Winegardner envied Southern writers, who thrive when they're identified as regional writers. Southerners, he argued, embrace their region's heritage and support their writers. Midwesterners don't.

Winegardner's essay despaired of finding a path forward. Yet even then, he and other novelists were exploring a new regional identity, a Midwestern-ness more intriguing than the provincial boosterism mocked in Sinclair Lewis' *Babbitt.* Novels such as Jeffrey Eugenides' *Middlesex* and *Crooked River Burning* shared a sense of loss and abandon common to the industrial cities of the Great Lakes States. Rust Belt literature, it's now being called—fiction preoccupied with a vast loss that left scars on landscapes and psyches, a longing for a golden era that will not return.

The phrase "Rust Belt" was coined 30 years ago, after the 1982 recession, to evoke the damage globalization inflicted on the industrial Upper Midwest. It evolved from "Rust Bowl," a comparison to the 1930s Dust Bowl, and it imitates "Bible Belt," H.L. Mencken's 1920s nickname for the South. But its opposite is "Sun Belt," the 1940s-vintage term for the South and the growing Southwest.

Like many aging epithets, the phrase "Rust Belt" is being reclaimed. It's acquired some cultural cachet recently thanks to the concept of "Rust Belt Chic," which celebrates Midwestern cities' history, architecture, and ethnic heritage. So it's a good time to check in with Winegardner, who is writing about Ohio again.

Much of his new novel in progress, tentatively titled *Red-Blooded American Smut*, is set in Northeast Ohio in the 1970s. Like *Crooked River Burning*, which traced Cleveland's decline from the Indians' 1948 World Series victory to the 1969 Cuyahoga River fire, his new novel is inspired by historic events here, from the life of Reuben Sturman, who ran a pornography empire from Cleveland, to the Kent State University shootings. I spoke with Winegardner about whether the concept of Rust Belt literature might provide a way out of the Midwestern writer's trap.

Q: Has anything changed since your "Toward A Literature of the Midwest" essay? If you start identifying Rust Belt literature as an idea, does it offer a possible way out of the limitations you identified 10 years ago?

A: I think it's an interesting idea that holds a lot of promise. The Midwest is nice and perceived as bland, so the idea of pitching what's going on in those states as Rust Belt rather than Midwest gives it a much sharper definition. It gives you a little more of an identity and an underclass identity.

The challenge is for some writer to better define what that means and make a case for it. The notion calls for a polemic, a broadside. For Rust Belt Lit to exist as a thing that's not a gentle pejorative, there needs to be some sense of how it would be connected to sales and prestige. That's the challenge, or no one would want to be identified with it. It'd have to be identified and hammered at enough that no one who was called that would see it as an insult.

It's one of things I was talking about in the first essay. "We see this as regional book, we see this as a Midwestern book," is code for "A New York publisher will not be getting behind it." "Rust Belt literature" would probably sound no different to the normative publicist in New York. The need for it to really be an attractive term has as much to do with getting writers to warm to the notion as it does with developing a readership that's loyal to it.

There are niches of American lit which definitely mean sales. I referred to Southern lit in the essay. It's still true. There are fewer independent bookstores than there were when I wrote that, but there are still book clubs all over the South that read exclusively Southern writers.

Q: How does the downtrodden-ness of the Rust Belt help Rust Belt literature?

A: It's not a conquered nation the way the South was, but it is a place that's not the main stage of American life. It's not the economic power it once was. There's a lot of poverty and desperation and fear. There's poverty and desperation and fear everywhere, but it less defines San Francisco than it does Gary, Indiana. It less defines New York than it does Cleveland. I think that's utterly different from what it was like to be from Cleveland in 1960.

A lot of literature comes from underclass people. In some ways, this is Frank O'Connor's argument in *The Lonely Voice*. He's talking about short fiction. His exact turn of phrase is, it comes from submerged population groups. There's a degree to which the Midwest is a submerged population group.

When you can't make fun anymore in a Sinclair Lewis way, I think there's great opportunity. That may be the thing that's changed most from when I wrote the essay. "Midwestern" still seemed nice and striving and earnest and easy to make fun of, in a way you make fun of the sloganeering chamber of commerce sensibility in the Midwest. It isn't gone, but it's sad now. Making fun of sad things is just mean. It's not art.

There's an opportunity for our stories and the niche they occupy to be presented in a way that's news. We're not Sinclair Lewis's Midwest.

We're not the chamber of commerce Midwest anymore either, despite what the chamber of commerce would have you believe. We're the Rust Belt, and bad stuff has happened to us, we have stories to tell, and we're not dead yet.

So much of Southern literature come from that impulse: "You conquered us, but fuck you." It's more, "Fuck New York, let's read about ourselves, let's support our people, let's make it a real priority to read the books." The Midwest still doesn't have that kind of swagger, but it's the kind of thing that can be championed in a non-boosterish way.

Q: Twelve years ago you were afraid the Midwest would never pull off a support for Midwestern literature that didn't come off as chamber-of-commerce boosterish.

A: It's still my fear, that it would still seem too much like you're trying too hard. But that was part of the whole polemic in the first place: Why should we have to try too hard? There's been this enormous amount of talent to come from the Midwest.

Q: Did Midwestern writers, even going back decades, have something in common?

A: A sense of being an outsider. It's the through-line of all those canonical Midwestern writers. Hemingway wrote from the vantage point of someone who felt very at home at the cool kids' party, but there's a deeply Midwestern stripe to him. Frederic, when he gets blown up in *A Farewell to Arms*, is making macaroni and cheese. There is that sense of Hemingway trying too hard, the way we think of Midwesterners when they do assimilate into some high culture and high society.

Gatsby—what a profoundly Midwestern [character]. He comes from Minnesota, he completely re-imagines himself by virtue of going east. Nick Carraway also comes from the Midwest, and he sees all of it from such a great vantage point, but he hightails it back to the Midwest to try to make sense of what happened to him when he was in New York.

Who can be the ultimate smart outsider on the fringe of things telling a story than Nick Carraway? The way Fitzgerald writes seems very Midwestern: We're outsiders, but we're not too far outsiders.

Q: In Cleveland, a panel discussion on how to write about the city became a debate about cheerleading versus criticism. One speaker was critical enough that one of the cheerleaders said, "Why don't you move? I'll help you move!"

A: See, there's a problem. No one would ever say that about someone writing a novel set in Brooklyn. That's a fundamentally art-destroying impulse. Art tends to sneak up behind things and pull their pants down, Harlem Globetrotters-ish. Art throws a spitball at the teacher.

That kind of boosterism is never going to really be art. The point isn't positive versus negative. It's truth versus lies. You're certainly not going to tell the story of the Rust Belt from the 1960s onward and have it be, "Hooray, Erie!"

Q: How is *Crooked River Burning* a Rust Belt book?

A: Boy, how is it not a Rust Belt book? In the years when I lived in Cleveland, I saw various things about how prosperous Cleveland was in the 20th century. It wasn't a place people made fun of, even as late as the early '60s. How did we get here from there?

I was researching, and I came across that *Ebony* article [that called] Cleveland the best place in America for a Negro to live. Boy, to go from an article like that in *Ebony* in 1950 to, less than 20 years later, America's second major race riot, how does that happen?

Crooked River Burning traces the transition of Cleveland and the Rust Belt from being the earnest, prosperous place it was right after the war to being something that could fairly be called the Rust Belt. The rust was just starting to clad the metal.

Q: How is your new book also a Rust Belt book?

A: It's not entirely set in Cleveland, though a very large percentage of it is. If Kent counts as Cleveland, then an even larger percentage. It's further down those rusty I-beams, the '70s and '80s. While it hops around in time, [it covers] the sort of malaise that happens in the Rust Belt in the '70s.

Red-Blooded American Smut is the working title. It's a fictionalized version of Reuben Sturman. It's based very loosely on his empire. In real life, Reuben Sturman's porn empire was a precursor of casinos in Rust Belt cities. It was a sin-based economy that was employing a lot of people who would otherwise been making a whole lot less money or none at all.

Q: In what ways is Jeffrey Eugenides a Rust Belt writer?

A: Both Jonathan Franzen's *The Corrections* and Eugenides' *Middlesex* came out about the same time at *Crooked River Burning*. They're all three very Rust Belt books. I think the best parts of *Middlesex* have to do with the fall of Detroit, the way Detroit changes in the '60s.

Q: If the term "Rust Belt writer" is launching, who else should be part of the canon?

A: Dean Bakopoulos. His *Please Don't Come Back From the Moon* is a little surreal, one degree beyond realism. There are all these fathers in Detroit who just disappear. Economic forces really fractured a lot of families in certain industrial cities. People had a hard time selling their house, and the dad would leave to go get a job in Houston. That was a lot of people's stories. Dean, as his name would indicate, is a Detroit Greek, an immigrant community that really dug in and thrived economically in downtown Detroit and [then] suffered. They had a real economic stake in how the city did.

Q: You talked at one point about infrastructures of support for literature. What's necessary for the Rust Belt to develop those infrastructures?

A: One really hip, smart website that could figure out a way to garner influence and feature really intelligent interviews with writers. You could convince both writers and publishers that it's an important thing, that it's great for your book if you're interviewed on this site. Writers, that'd be easy. We'll talk to anybody if we think it'll sell four books. Publishers, that's a lot harder.

One extraordinarily well done website could do what used to get done occasionally by one amazing independent book seller. Things like Goodreads have an economic impact. People check in on them. They link in to social media with it. You could do events, where you flew people in, if you got a couple of hundred people to show up routinely. People will come out for them. Then a publisher will fly a writer there, you can interview them, and put the interview on a website.

There are a good dozen readings and conferences like that in the South, from the Decatur Book Festival in Atlanta, which is huge, to the Southern Festival of Books to the Pirate's Alley Faulkner Society conference, which is bigger than just Faulkner. To my knowledge, the Rust Belt doesn't have one. Maybe a signature event is something that missing, something people would really turn out for.

You need a real online community that doesn't seem niche-y, doesn't seem boosterish, and isn't saying things like 'I'll help you move,' and is embracing things that tell the truth about the Rust Belt, rather than just create bumper stickers about the Rust Belt.

Dispatches from the Rust Belt

The Biggest Little-Known Book Award

Jacqueline Marino

No one stumbles upon the Anisfield-Wolf Book Award collection at the Cleveland Public Library. The books are shelved in three locked cabinets of the Treasure Room, a drum-tight chamber in Special Collections that also houses four other collections, including *1001 Arabian Nights* published in more than 60 languages and the Robin Hood tales.

The Treasure Room is a place most patrons never see, the only place where you can find all the winning volumes of Cleveland's venerated book prize.

Every September, Kelly Ross Brown, the librarian who maintains the collection, receives a few requests to see it. This is the time of year when jury chair Henry Louis Gates, Jr., arrives in Cleveland to present the winning authors with up to $10,000 each.

But most of the time, the Anisfield-Wolf corner of the Treasure Room remains unoccupied.

Celebrated as the only book award in America focused on issues of racism and diversity, the Anisfield-Wolf Book Award was created in 1934, when Cleveland and the rest of America were in the throes of Jim Crow. This was two decades before Brown vs. Board of Education declared school segregation unconstitutional, fueling the nascent Civil Rights Movement.

Its winner's circle is as profound as Pulitzer's: Martin Luther King, Jr., won the award in 1959, four years before giving his "I Have a

Dream" speech. Langston Hughes won it for *Simple Takes a Wife*. John Hersey won it for *The Wall*. John Howard Griffin for *Black Like Me*. Zadie Smith for *On Beauty*. Malcolm X has won it. Alex Haley has won it, as have Jonathan Kozol, Junot Díaz and Toni Morrison. In all, 216 works have won this singular award that speaks to both an author's literary skill and ability to convey a message of social justice.

Yet, for the majority of the award's 78-year history, most Clevelanders—and many in the literary world—have not known this prize even existed.

And many still don't.

As Ross Brown worked to unlock one of the cabinets, sunlight streamed in through a high window, warming the quiet space. I looked for the 2013 winners, particularly the one I had just read, Laird Hunt's *Kind One*, a fictional work about slavery that illuminates a rarely discussed truth: Oppressed people can and do oppress other people when given the opportunity.

Another group soon gathered outside the door, and I was asked to leave. In addition to housing the winners of Cleveland's esteemed book award, the Treasure Room has become a nice spot to hold meetings.

Very few turkeys

In popular culture, Clevelanders are suffering sports fans, weather-beaten cynics and victims of bizarrely sadistic criminals (Ariel Castro, Anthony Sowell, the Torso Murderer). We're not usually portrayed as smart folks known for our passion for literature or social justice, and the Anisfield-Wolf Book Award spotlights both. It awards exemplary writing, the kind that pushes you into self-examination. It is a call to reflection and discomfort, to discussions you didn't intend to bring up and can't stop thinking about after you do.

"Before anyone had heard of Gwendolyn Brooks, Langston Hughes or Nadine Gordimer, all had won Anisfield-Wolf prizes for their work," says Karen Long, the consultant who manages the award for The Cleveland Foundation. "While there have been a few turkeys, most of these books have set the table for the conversations our children will be having in the 21st century."

Despite being a substantial literary prize, for most of its history the award resembled the modesty of its founder, Edith Anisfield Wolf, (1889-1963), a Cleveland poet and philanthropist known for several books of poetry and many charitable activities. Described in a 1954 *Plain Dealer* article as "Cleveland's publicity-shy philanthropist," she nonetheless appeared in a number of articles for her civic work. She was active in the Women's City Club, the Association for Crippled and Disabled, and the Cleveland Branch of the American Society of Pen Women. She was also a board member of the Cleveland Public Library, whose collection includes copies of her correspondence regarding donations: a curtain for an auditorium here, printing costs for a manuscript there.

Wolf was approachable but discerning. One article called her "a generous but shrewd businesswoman who can spot a 'phony' every time."

On an average day in 1943, she could be found working in her victory garden at her home on East Boulevard, where her father had amassed one of the most valuable private libraries in the city, or in her office in the Union Commerce Building, where she wrote her poetry and "homey" articles for women's magazines. In her poetry and her good works, Wolf championed equality and humanity. This one was chosen to accompany a list of the award winners:

Walls
Countries are such funny things
With language, law, tariff, borders;
Immigration, customs, orders;
Army, navy, patrol on wings;
When we've all the wide world
To live in as brothers-
Our hug-ed prejudice unfurled
To understand each others'

Wolf was the only child of John Anisfield, a Jewish immigrant who came to Cleveland from Vienna as a teenager and worked his way up in the garment industry to start his own business, The John Anisfield Company. By the early 1900s, it employed 700 people. A 1929 obituary says he became "one of the best-known clothing manufacturers of the country."

Anisfield retired in 1923 to devote all his time to philanthropy. He had been president of Mount Sinai Hospital, known for treating patients of all religions and races. He established a camp for poor children and a society that made loans without interest.

"He accepted the leadership of every charitable undertaking he could and gave unsparingly of his time and money to the promotion of better living, especially among members of his own race, the Jews," his obit reads.

Young Edith began sharing her father's interest in social causes at age 12. "He encouraged her to come into his office every Saturday to help him administer his philanthropic interests," says Mary Louise Hahn, who managed the Anisfield-Wolf Book Awards from 1995 until this year and has researched Wolf's life.

Quietly building steam

In 1934, after long talks with her friend, Amy Loveman, an editor at the *Saturday Review of Literature*, Wolf established The John Anisfield Award to reflect her family's dedication to social justice. There is little about the early decades of the award in the library file or at the Cleveland Foundation, which began administering the award after Wolf's death in 1963.

Ross Brown recently turned up a 1959 Florida State University master's thesis by V. Leslie Thomson that chronicled the development and examined the significance of the award-winning books. Thomson corresponded with Wolf and quotes an unpublished paper by another author, Western Reserve University library student Fay P. Armstrong, who had access to Wolf's personal files. In her paper, written in 1951, Armstrong compiled the first complete list of award-winning books.

According to Armstrong, the first John Anisfield Award was to be given to "a sound and significant book published either in the United States or abroad in the previous twelve months on a subject of race relations in the contemporary world."

The first jurors were Henry Seidel Canby, editor of the *Saturday Review of Literature*; Henry Pratt Fairchild, sociology professor at New

York University; and Donald Young of the Social Service Research Council. The award went to Harold F. Gosnell for *Negro Politicians: The Rise of Negro Politics in Chicago*. The prize was $1,000, a substantial amount at that time.

In 1941, after the award was given to Louis Adamic's *From Many Lands*, a work the judges described as close to fiction, they recommended a second award be given for creative literature. In a letter to Wolf, Canby explained "the so-called scholarly award would lend importance and dignity to the creative literary book, which being in all probability more popular would in turn help to carry the more serious work."

When the new award was announced in 1942, it was made clear that the creative work "must perform an outstanding service in clarifying the problems of racial relations, whether it be in the area of fiction, drama, poetry, biography or autobiography." The total award amount increased to $2,000 and was not necessarily split equally between the two winners, according to Thomson.

Over time, the jury included some of the most recognized names in literature and the humanities, including author Pearl Buck, historian Oscar Handlin, novelist Lillian Smith and poet Gwendolyn Brooks. For decades, the jury was chaired by Princeton anthropologist Ashley Montagu.

After the death of her husband, the lawyer Eugene Everett Wolf, in 1944, Edith Anisfield Wolf added his name to the award.

Dispatches from the Rust Belt

Aaron Dilloway's Walls Of Noise: Hanson Records

Zoe Gould

"**W**e had a popcorn and pizza party here last night," Aaron Dilloway apologizes as he picks up stray kernels and straightens up the shop before his day begins. The owner and founder of Hanson Records, Dilloway is not your stereotypical noise rocker. The pizza and popcorn party was for his kids, a six-year-old boy and two-year-old girl. His open face and unassuming, relaxed demeanor clashes with the mysterious and eccentric image that noise music evokes. But aside from his incredible success in the world of noise and experimental music, Aaron runs and operates his record store and label from the second floor of a commercial building on College Street—the main drag of Oberlin, Ohio.

Hanson Records, much like Dilloway himself, is simple at first glance. The walls are lined with neat rows of records and Lou Reed posters, books on John Cage scatter the shelves, and Hanson Records t-shirts are tacked to the wall behind the counter. A potted plant sits on the floor next to a speaker playing atmospheric music that compels the shoppers to browse and, hopefully, to buy. But the charm of Hanson lies in the details. Where the mountains of classic rock and Joan Baez LPs would be in your average record store, Hanson is stocked with experimental, noise, and old school punk. And the memorabilia is books of Bryan Lewis Saunders self-portraits, all drawn while under some drug, from valium-induced frizz to swooping and painful lines inspired by two squirts of computer duster. The music may be ambient, but Aaron handpicks it rather than let his computer self-generate an amiable playlist.

The store's niche starts to become clear.

Even so, Aaron swivels his head effortlessly to take a look at whoever walks in the door, giving them a smiling and practiced, "Let me know if I can help you find anything." He has a patient and effortless brand of friendliness. Donning muted, casual button-downs and cardigans, he could be any age between twenty-eight and forty. Even his light brown hair with a small thinning patch doesn't seem to age his young spirit. By his wrist lies a small thunderbolt tattoo, thick and sharp like the ones you'd find in a Flash comic book. As a sign of both reticence and revelry, as we talk he is always willing to drop a needle on any album in the store to let the music speak for itself.

Noise and experimental music are recent genres—born out of radical punk movements and the underbelly of glam rock fame. Born in 1976, Aaron Dilloway entered the world at the right time to witness the growth of the experimental.

He grew up in South Lyon, Michigan, the youngest of three kids, with his siblings nearly ten years ahead of him. His older brother played hockey and rode BMX bikes, a vision of Midwestern athleticism, and tortured the records he had ceased to enjoy. "He hung a tire from the ceiling in the basement and put records he didn't like inside in it and shot slapshots at them," until they were satisfactorily smashed. "One day," Aaron chuckled, "I came home and my Kiss record was shattered. I was so upset and my mom felt really bad so she took me to the mall to buy new ones."

By 1984, the family had moved to Brighton, Michigan, a small suburb outside of Ann Arbor. Aaron came across punk music in the same way that most kids find the new underground trend—someone's sister. "She was the coolest person I'd ever seen" Aaron describes, measuring his hands above his head to illustrate the approximate height of her hair. She showed them the Butthole Surfers—"we were all crackin' up cause of the name"—and his fascination with punk was planted. As he grew up, Dilloway dragged himself across Ann Arbor record shops, sopping up new music and looking for live shows. What he found was The Lab, a house of punk rock enthusiasts who held rowdy shows in the basement; Aaron would later move into a similar house in the mid-90s to start Hanson Records.

The Lab was the hub of the Ann Arbor punk scene and, in many ways, the seed of the noise movement—at least for Aaron Dilloway. When the store is empty, Aaron leans back in his office chair and recounts what he still considers to be "the funnest day" of his life. It reads like a Midwestern version of an Alice Cooper song: "We skateboarded all day, got chased by the cops and had to split up. When we all eventually found each other again, we went to Ann Arbor." They had heard that The Laughing Hyenas were playing at The Lab, and that Couch, unknown to them, would be opening. Couch, Aaron recalls, was "straight noise, hit you like a wall of sound." In his mimicked reaction, his eyes bulge as he puts his shaking hands out to stop the onslaught. Perusing a record store in the following weeks, he came across a Couch album and immediately bought it, thinking, "How could this band have a record?" He was shocked that he recognized some of their songs from the live show. Mesmerized by the idea that Couch's chaotic barrage of noise was a composed and replicable song, Aaron went back to the store and demanded more music just like it.

The albums that followed would be Aaron's entryway into the experimental. In his store, he still keeps copies of many of the albums that he found in his teenage years. Aaron has three albums by Caroliner, a band who adds to their name, and their roster, with every album that they release. For one album, they were Caroliner Rainbow Splinter Mind Deserves, and for another, Caroliner Rainbow Hernia Milk Queen. Chuckling and eager to share the off-brand humor, Aaron brings over two of their records to show me. Each one is wrapped in a different form of makeshift sleeve, "this one is made out of an adult diaper wrapper," he says, and it's closed with a Caroliner sticker. The first Caroliner record he bought came in a box filled with moldy newspaper and other junk. Galvanized by the band's humor and sound, Aaron reveled in the mysterious and unapologetic quality of bands like Caroliner. "It was music, but it was indescribable," he remembers. "What rubbed me the wrong way about academic experimental music is that the mystery is gone."

In the early 1990s, Aaron and his friends abandoned their grunge band chords in pursuit of that inexplicable sound. They teamed up with a girl from their high school—"Oh, you play the oboe? How weird! Wanna be in our band?"—and Galen was born. Aaron, by now an exposed sentimentalist, still has the Toxic Shock catalog that he used to order random albums from by name alone, consequently getting turned on to bands from Japan and Switzerland. For all the angst and subversion of punk and experimental music, there is a real camaraderie between members of the underground; the randomness of their band names celebrates a commitment to shattering the predictable. They were soldiers of confusion, and they were armed with a new brand of noise.

Aaron and the rest of Galen saved up the money to self-press a record when Bulb Records (Couch's label) offered to distribute if Galen could cover the cost of pressing the LPs. After putting an ad in *Bananafish*, another music index, he started getting letters and orders from around the world. "I had all these new pen pals," he says and smiles. Galen was the first band to release an LP with Hanson Records in 1994, and by '96 Hanson had released the albums of three other artists, friends of Galen and travelling artists in the Ann Arbor underground.

After a few years touring with Galen, two of the members moved to New York City for college, and the band dissolved into smaller, more transient projects. Aaron "got tired of playing strange guitar. I wanted to play chords again." He had already been finding tapes and recording over them for years when his friend Nate Young presented a tape called Wolf Eyes by Paul Winter and another of Robert Redford reading Peter and the Wolf, with a B-side of howling realistic wolf cries. Nate taped over Wolf Eyes with a mixture of organ sounds and wolf howling from the Redford tape and named the new project, fittingly, Wolf Eyes. Aaron started playing guitar on Nate's recordings and quickly became a lasting member of the group, his last band affiliation before his solo career.

For seven years, Dilloway helped Wolf Eyes gain critical acclaim—something that most, if not all, noise bands never achieve. Written up in publications like *Spin* and *The Wire*, Wolf Eyes saw an unprecedented amount of daylight for a predominantly underground band. *Pitchfork*, another widely read site for popular and new music, wrote that in the early aughts, Wolf Eyes was "the most visible band in the international noise scene." They were "the face of noise for a generation," shaping public perception of what had previously been an unknown and deeply misunderstood genre.

Touring with bands like Sonic Youth and Andrew W.K. boosted Wolf Eyes' listenership while simultaneously (and nearly singlehandedly) dragging noise music into the limelight. But they did not submit to the hype. Wolf Eyes churned out hundreds of unabashedly eclectic songs that incorporated heavy industrial beats, loose noise, and messily ominous undertones. But because of their infectious energy and authentically experimental spirit, Wolf Eyes became one of "the most important experimental bands in the world." Aaron Dilloway had reached the top.

In 2005, he left for Nepal to accompany his wife during her field research. By the time he returned, Wolf Eyes was gearing up to tour again, and he bowed out in an almost romantic gesture, letting the band go on without him. Mike Connelly had joined in his absence and Dilloway was admittedly reluctant to pick up and travel again. Instead, he left the band, which would go on to reap the benefits of fame for another seven years.

Modest to the point of erasure, Aaron told me nothing about Wolf Eyes' staggering success. He appears to have escaped the spotlight unscathed, devoid of any distasteful grasping for his glory days. Which is not to say that Wolf Eyes was the peak of Aaron's career. In fact, his most prized work was still six years away.

The last album we listen to together is at my request, a spoken word collection of William Burroughs recordings. One of which, "Origin and Theory of Tape Cut-ups" happens to be part of the manifesto of noise music; Dilloway himself covered its importance in a music-related Podcast. Burroughs' deep, surprisingly nerdy, voice details the collaging of language and sound: cutting into things with the intention of rearranging them. What emerges, he says, can sometimes predict the future: "when you cut into the present, the future leaks out." The ultimate trick has been played when your randomness reinvents itself. This notion is central to the experimental nature of noise music. Aaron also describes his songwriting process as a study in deviation: "I have a skeleton of what I'll do … within that skeleton there's a lot of improv, and it depends on the vibe, where it will go." Trusting the artist to pull the music where it needs to go is the progressive and empowering side of noise. "How random is random?" Burroughs philosophizes; when is your unconscious mind pulling a fast one on your reasoning, letting you believe you have the power to surprise yourself? *Modern Jester*, Aaron's biggest musical accomplishment to date, toys with these central ideas.

Released in 2011, *Modern Jester* took roughly five years from concept to finish. Beginning before the birth of his son, and ending just after the birth of his daughter, *Modern Jester* is the culmination of Aaron's recent work. It is a feat of trickery, at once mysterious and personal, dark and funny. Aaron's wife, a Professor of Anthropology at Oberlin

College, and his son and daughter, can all be found on the inside cover wearing masks or holding live snakes. The album is comprised of seven songs, two of which are eighteen minutes long. Each track buzzes and grates with static, while balancing the deep valleys of gulping subwoofers and melodic, frenzied beeps. He pointed me to track four, "Body Chaos," an eighteen-minute epic of loops interrupted by and interrupting scattered explosions of organic tape recordings. Each field recording has been peeled from reality and shaken, stretched, and scratched into original sounds. While I am timid to suggest anything about the overarching meaning of the tones (taking Aaron's advice about the value of explanation), "Body Chaos" embraces the notion of a perpetually impending, tumbling, and improvised future.

Now, Aaron travels to weekend gigs almost once a month. Recently, his music has been featuring whistling and "tap dancing" (Aaron tapping his feet against his chair and other objects). Far from a stubbornly reflective musician, Dilloway keeps up to date with current noise and experimental music happening on campus. Hanson Records even becomes a venue every now and again, hosting students and travelling bands in its lobby at the top of the stairs. Dilloway has been talking with Tom Lopez, the Associate Professor of Computer and Digital Arts at Oberlin's Conservatory, about collaborating to produce LPs featuring compilations of student and faculty work.

Now that his wife's tenure has secured Oberlin as their long-term home, and Hanson Records has been well-received by students and locals, Aaron is enjoying his Dadly responsibilities and continues to seek new inspiration. Invisible to the untrained eye, Dilloway's presence has drawn noise and experimental talent from far and wide to the sleepy college town in search of collaboration.

To those who don't know Aaron's noise music prowess, Hanson is a run-of-the-mill record store. But a wall of complex and chaotic noise will blow back anybody willing to peer into Hanson Records' roots. And they just might come back for more.

A Sense of What a City Was: A History of Rust Belt Alt-Weeklies

Laura Putre

ike Superman in 1938, a big S emblazoned on his chest as he tears open his dress shirt—except substitute a swooping red E—the *Cleveland Edition* appeared in 1986. It was four years after the *Cleveland Press,* the scrappier of the city's two dailies, closed, leaving readers with the *Plain Dealer,* the fat suburban paper.

The *Edition* was an alt-weekly newspaper distributed in coffee shops, booksellers, and record stores. Its pages were packed with columns by writers who could carry, and sometimes levitate, a sentence: Eric Broder, whose absurdist, satirical humor column might have gone over in the early 1900s (think George Herriman's *Krazy Kat* or Don Marquis' *Archy and Mehitabel*), but wouldn't have lived a day in the corporate daily newspapers of the 1980s. Amy Sparks, who dauntingly wove poetic language and first-person writing into engaging art and culture critiques. Mark Winegardner, whose literary yet accessible columns made me read 1,400 words about sports from beginning to end, for the first and last time. Roldo's constant hammering away at the inner workings of City Hall—you'd find him camped out there, unassumingly overhearing people's conversations—made me care about the politics of downtown.

The *Edition* was also an incubator for young talent. Comic book artist Derf debuted his trademark strip "The City" in its pages. Martha Southgate, the young adult novelist, was an intern there. Even the receptionist, Meredith Rutledge, went on to bigger things: She's now a curator

41

at the Rock and Roll Hall of Fame.

When I found the *Edition*, around 1988, I was in college at Kent State, and for the first time I dared to think that I could live in Cleveland and be a writer. In the southwest suburbs where I grew up, everyone's dad was a vacuum cleaner engineer. Though we went camping a lot, I'd never been to a Cleveland Orchestra concert, only set foot in University Circle a couple of times. Coventry and the Cedar Lee Theater were apparitions to me. I was working on a journalism degree, and had written a handful of music reviews for *Alternative Press*, but the PD didn't seem like a place that would hire me—I wasn't interested in hard news. I didn't have money or connections to try New York or Chicago. Thanks to the *Edition*, I finally knew there were writers in Cleveland, and art galleries that didn't traffic in Thomas Kinkade paintings. And the *Edition* itself might be a place you could go to get your first writing job, if you had a roommate and were willing to take a second job in a bookstore.

Chris Potter, editor of the *Pittsburgh City Paper*, had a similar alt-weekly experience. The Rust Belt wasn't like the big coastal cities, or even Chicago, where the cultural and political life of the city is inescapable. The racial politics, the economic inequality, and the post-punk bands were there, but you had to work to find them. You had to take three buses to get there, instead of hopping on a subway.

Potter grew up outside of Pittsburgh in the suburb of Upper Saint Clair. "It was basically the political birthing place of Rick Santorum," he says. As a teen, he'd take the bus into the city, and pick up an alternative weekly newspaper called *In Pittsburgh*. In the city, "there were things, you kind of knew you weren't in Kansas any more," he recalls. "One of those things was the alt-weekly paper. It would help you feel your way around the city."

When Potter graduated from college, one of the first things he did was send his writing clips to *In Pittsburgh*. "I got a gig writing art reviews at first, because basically I wasn't too proud. I think my first story, I was writing about performance-art groups, these guys were walking around in shallow pools wearing hip waders. There were live lobsters and shit. It actually turned out to be pretty instructive because covering city council, it turns out, is not that much different. For me, it was the first time I had a sense of what a city was."

Potter ended up working at *In Pittsburgh* and later joined *Pittsburgh City Paper*, his current employer. By the time I was back in Cleveland looking for a writing gig, the *Edition* was gone. I spent my early newspaper career at the *Free Times*, a spinoff of the *Edition*. Like Potter, I covered the stories nobody else wanted, because I was the new kid. I then worked at *Cleveland Scene* during the time the paper was owned by a Phoenix-based chain called *New Times*. Crime and salacious stories ruled at the *New Times*-era Scene. I was grateful for the paycheck at both places. But I kept searching for the spark, the liveliness and sense of fun, the smart-meets-subversive attitude I saw in the *Edition*. Even later, when I was editor of a weekly paper in Chicago—and now, helping start up Belt—I am still pursuing the *Edition* I read in college. I'll let you know if ever I find it.

§

Bill Gunlocke, a Lakewood English teacher and bookstore clerk, started the *Edition* with an inheritance from his dad's office furniture company in rural New York. One day at Gunlocke's bookstore, a customer walked in wearing a *New York* magazine shirt. "I thought to myself, 'What publication in Cleveland would I wear the T-shirt of? None.'"

Gunlocke started thinking about starting a publication he wanted to read. At the downtown library, he studied up on alternative weekly newspapers in other cities: the *Boston Phoenix*, the *Chicago Reader*. "I thought hell, I could do one of these. I'm a mix of a lot of things. Not a genius or an expert at any of them, but I knew enough books, enough music, enough politics." He sent himself to a New York publishing conference, where he blew off most of the sessions ("I spent a lot of time just walking around New York"). Between skipping talks at the conference, Gunlock befriended a magazine designer named Greg Paul who happened to be from Cleveland, too. Together, they got to work on a clean yet punchy design for the *Edition*.

Gunlocke rented some office space above the Publix bookstore on Huron Road, and hired his first employee, Eric Broder, who had recently received a journalism master's from University of Michigan. Even more importantly, the girls Gunlocke knew thought that Broder was funny.

"Neither of us are hard-chargers," says Gunlocke of himself

and Broder. "At the time, we were flying blind."

The pair hung out in the office for a good year and a half, says Broder, before they put out a paper. "We had to wait for the design—that took a long time," says Broder. "It seemed to take forever."

Broder's first column was about the Beatles. "It was like, 'To hell with the Beatles, they're no good.' It was one of the dumbest things that has ever been written. I just wasn't into them. I liked the Rolling Stones. 'They were of their time, I guess. They're not cool. They don't rock.'"

"The people who got it, got it," he says of his column. "And the people who didn't just thought I was an asshole."

Gunlocke noticed that the other cities' weeklies had arts and entertainment listings. "That seemed to be the mantra, you had to have good listings. If you had good listings, then no matter your cover story, people would be in the habit of picking it up.

"There was a template, no question. Every city did it just the same. Except we did ours a little different, to be honest. Our design was better looking than the other papers; the other papers even told us that."

Gunlocke wasn't interested in hiring reporters to write "boffo cover stories." He was interested in columnists, people who were obsessed with their subjects—Doug Clarke from the old *Cleveland Press* on sports, environmentalist David Beach on the lakefront. "It became a little more writerly than the standard weekly—more individual voices. I used to say, 'Small as we are, non-profitable as we are, if there were a media softball league in Cleveland, everybody would recognize our starting lineup because they week after week had their own column. It was a team of individuals and I liked that.'"

But he didn't know how to sell it. The *Edition* ran out of money and closed twice, reopening when Gunlocke rounded up some more cash, and then closed for good in 1992. "I was so not a salesman," he says. "I didn't know how to cut through the bullshit. I just thought this Baby Boom we represented in our minds—and who the advertisers were more likely to want because they'd graduated from college and those kinds of things—we would just naturally bring in ads from places like the Cedar Lee. I never got one from the Cedar Lee. [Cedar Lee owner] John Foreman said to me once, 'If we advertise in your paper, we'll look like an arts theater and we just don't want to be thought of as an arts theater.' And I thought, 'You're kidding me.' I should have just rolled up the tent then. If somebody's going to use that kind of logic not to advertise in the fucking weekly paper, what the hell? What town have we got?"

Another weekly paper, a tabloid called *Scene*, fared better as a business. Started by gas station owner Rich Kabat with a family loan, *Scene* struck gold by covering the minutia of the acts playing at rock and blues clubs in town with an approach that was more boosterish than critical. An era-appropriate comparison: *Scene* was the wildly popular Bob Seger to the *Edition*'s self-defeating Replacements.

At the *Edition*, compiling the weekly arts and entertainment listings sucked up a lot of time. "And we still didn't get the ads. Those people went to *Scene*. Really? We used to think, 'Really? You're gonna put it in *Scene*? But *Scene* had their obsession. They really gave a shit who was playing at these clubs. I mean, they really, really gave a shit and we didn't.

"So they got the ads that we wanted and we thought we deserved because we were better and we were better overall, but they cared about their niche and they wore black silk baseball jackets with some band on the back and it was cheesy looking, but it mattered."

§

In 1965, an upstart Detroit paper called *Fifth Estate* was started by a politically astute 17-year-old named Harvey Ovshinsky, working out of his dad's basement in suburban Bloomfield Hills. In 2015, *Fifth Estate* will celebrates its fiftieth anniversary as perhaps the longest continuously published underground newspaper (although now it's a twice-yearly magazine rather than a weekly or biweekly newspaper).

After a summer internship at the underground *Los Angeles Free Press*, Ovshinsky wanted to get his own protest paper going at home, so he recruited a couple of his friends.

"Maybe that idea of zeitgeist was overused, but it really was what drove us," recalls Peter Werbe, a *Fifth Estate* staff member since the beginning and longtime host of a leftist radio talk show. "The idea that teenagers and people in their early twenties could put out a newspaper was foreign—they were big, expensive operations—but literally with a portable manual typewriter, some glue and a kitchen table, you could produce a newspaper."

The first issue, which ran four pages and was given away at concerts and at college campuses, announced that itself as "Detroit's New Progressive Biweekly Newspaper." It included an interview with a disillusioned U.S. soldier who had just returned from two years in Vietnam, and an editorial by Ovshinksy earnestly declaring "We are the fifth [estate] because we are something different than Detroit's other newspapers. We hope to fill a void ... created by party-controlled newspapers and the cutting of those articles which might express the more liberal viewpoint. That's what we really are—the voice (I hate that word) of the liberal element of Detroit."

The paper moved to a space in Detroit's burgeoning "hippie district," a development on historic Plum Street put together by a local entrepreneur named Robert Cobb. "When we moved down there, because of the nature of the times, [the paper] really took off," Werbe recalls. "Here was this anti-capitalist paper, and it really owed its success and entrepreneurship to a capitalist who had little interest in the content."

Circulation was helped by the Keep on Trucking Collective, some friends of the paper who had landed the Detroit distribution rights to *Rolling Stone*. Store owners who wanted to carry *Rolling Stone* also had to carry *Fifth Estate* and several other radical papers. "They'd say, 'I don't want to take this commie newspaper,' 'Well, you've gotta take it all or none.' We wound up in stores all over the place," says Werbe.

Kids and homeless people, along with Werbe and a few other staffers, sold papers on the street for 15 cents and kept the money. The main staffers drew a weekly salary of $35, plus the street sales. "It sounds like we're talking about the 1910s, selling newspapers for 15 cents and being able to live on it," says Werbe. "But we lived in an apartment, our rent was like $60 a month, and you could buy an old junker car for 50 bucks. You had young people freed up to work on the *Fifth Estate*. Now if you're 20 years old, you're thinking 'I've got to get two jobs to buy my junker car for $4,000.'"

Werbe describes the paper in its early days as a "movement publication. It chronicled all the resistance movements of the era, primarily anti-war but certainly civil rights, civil liberties." It was a voice of resistance to the Vietnam War, but it was also pro-G.I.—and the staff worked hard to get the paper into the hands of soldiers. *Fifth Estate* sent reporters into combat zones in Vietnam to interview soldiers on both sides.

In 1967, riots broke on Detroit's Northwest Side after police in an African-American neighborhood arrested revelers at a party for two returning Vietnam veterans. Violence and looting spread to surrounding areas, and after five days, 43 people were dead and more than 7,000 had been arrested. Werbe and Ovshinsky were out on the streets taking photographs of the looters, some of whom were cops. A tear-gas grenade was thrown through the office window. Some suspect the grenade was thrown by the police or National Guard soldiers in retaliation for the photographs of cops looting, and the paper's larger coverage of the riot, which included printing a memo from an Air National Guard commander imploring guardsmen to stop looting.

The guardsmen had set up camp at some of the area high schools. "Harvey and I went over to my high school alma mater, Central High School in Detroit, and—because we had to fight for them—we actually had Detroit police press credentials. So we rolled up to the checkpoint at the high school, and I said, 'Hi, we're from the press.' He said, 'Let me see your press credentials, and this guy looked at me and raised his M-1 Garand and said, 'I know who you are. Get outta here.'"

By the early 1970s, Ovshinsky had left *Fifth Estate*. He had registered as a conscientious objector, and thought the paper's views were becoming too radical. Werbe and some other staffers, however, thought *Fifth Estate* was going soft, so they staged a peaceful takeover, refusing to take ads any longer. They declared the *Fifth Estate* an anarchist paper. Coverage in the 1990s included a takedown of unions during a Detroit newspaper strike, which didn't go over very well in the labor capital of the world.

"I think that [the union coverage] is fairly complex and fairly nuanced, and getting it out in a couple of sentences is difficult," says Werbe of the controversy over the newspaper strike, "but as revolutionaries who were interested in overthrowing capitalism, we were saying what institutions were an impediment to that. One of them was these institutions of unions—that were almost by their very nature conservative and accepted the definitions and parameters of capitalism."

Fifth Estate has since mellowed. "We don't make any real combative critiques any longer," says Werbe. "Not of people who are involved in protests and resistances. Because I just want to see, what are people doing for reforms, to improve people's lives, to help people. It's pretty easy to be critical. We were almost critical of everything."

Today the paper, describing itself as an "anarchist, anti-capitalist, anti-authoritarian, anti-profit project" focuses strictly on national and international coverage. (Online, it's organized into two sections: "Contents" and "Anarchy Section.") Its circulation has never topped 20,000. "It was the publication of a community," says Werbe. "We never saw it like that, but it was the voice of a particular community with a particular set of beliefs that were annunciated and reaffirmed every week."

§

During the 1990s, Pittsburgh had competing alternative news-weeklies. *In Pittsburgh* literally rose from the castoffs of the steel industry in the 1980s. Founder John Burstin used profits from his scrap-metal business to start the paper because he believed the city needed a liberal voice. "[Burstin] came at it from an activist point of view," recalls Charlie Humphrey, editor of *In Pittsburgh* in the 1980s, now working for two Pittsburgh arts non-profits. "I think he had a vision for how the alternative press could impact a community."

The writers, recalls Humphrey, "all really understood the importance of the alternative voice—while the journalism and reporting is rigorous, the actual voice of the writing is of a real sentient human being who is experiencing this. It does away with some of the stylistic conventions you see in the daily media. We were writing in a tone native in its snarkiness, and people of a certain age, they could identify with that."

A weekly column called "Eyesores" profiled a run-down building in the city and how it got that way. One cover story, titled "Trajectories," catalogued all the war monuments depicting guns and cannons in the city and calculated—according to the caliber of the gun and the ordnance it carried—where a shot would land if the symbolic weapon were fired.

In 1990, a businessman from Colorado named Brad Witherell started the *City Paper*. Witherell owned interests in Pittsburgh-area Christmas tree farms, fireworks warehouses, and phone sex hotlines. He started the *City Paper* after *In Pittsburgh* decided to stop running phone sex ads.

"You had these two papers who were just the yin and yang of alternative journalism," says *City Paper* editor Chris Potter, "high-minded liberal and revenue-based." Both alt-weeklies got a windfall in 1992, when the two daily papers, the *Press* and the *Post-Gazette*, went on strike. Advertisers migrated to the alternative weeklies, and some never left.

Potter worked at *In Pittsburgh* from 1995 to 1997. During that time, the paper mounted a big investigation into police accountability after a black motorist died at the hands of suburban police inside the city limits. "What we found when we did some stories, was there were people from all walks of life, whites as well as blacks, who had these sort of experiences with police," says Potter. "We took a strong advocacy position on the creation of a citizen review board, calling for the oversight of the department. I don't think there was anybody in town paying attention to that in the way that we were. We turned up individual cases where this had happened that had slipped under everybody else's radar."

Potter left for *City Paper* in 1997, when Philadelphia-based Review Publishing bought *In Pittsburgh*. The paper had been critical of then Mayor Tom Murphy's pro-downtown investment strategy. One night not long after the sale, the new owners of *In Pittsburgh* were invited to two parties—Murphy's reelection victory party or that of the supporters of the police department citizen review board, which was on the same ballot. "Our new owners went to the mayor's victory party, so we saw the handwriting on the wall," says Potter. *In Pittsburgh* struggled to keep up with the competition for a few years. In 2001, the *City Paper* bought its rival and shut it down.

Potter and his colleagues brought to the *City Paper* coverage critical of the mayor and his love affair with downtown retail, which included a multimillion dollar tax incentive for a new Lazarus department store. In 1998, the *City Paper* staff met with the editors of the *Cleveland Free Times* and the *Cincinnati CityBeat* and hatched a plan for a collaborative series on the public funding of sports stadiums. Cleveland already had Progressive, *nee* Jacobs Field and Quicken Loans *nee* Gund Arena. The *Edition*'s Roldo Bartimole had already spent years warning readers about the hollow promise of public money for wealthy sports team owners—to no avail. Pittsburgh was considering new sports facilities. The *Pittsburgh Post-Gazette*, which owned a piece of the Pittsburgh Pirates, was cautioning readers (which is to say, voters) that if Pittsburgh didn't fork over the cash for new arenas, their rival city to the northwest would beat them for good.

"We did this joint package deal where [all three alt-weeklies] had almost the exact same cover," Potter recalls. "It was three hot dogs with the names of the cities spelled out on them, and we had this thing where we showed the lineup in each city—who was playing which role, who was the pitchman." Each city's stadium financing lobbying campaign "was all coming out of the same playbook. Whether you're in the American or National League, it's the same game and they're telling you exactly the same shit."

"We found out Cincinnati had the worst deal of all of them," recalls John Fox, the *CityBeat* editor in Cincinnati at the time. "We compared how those things were funded, how much they cost, how much they were supposed to cost. It was a great series, though it didn't make any difference. The sales tax passed anyway, and the overruns were huge."

§

Fox, previously the editor of a mom-and-pop paper called *Everybody's News*, started *CityBeat* in 1994 with money from an investor named Tom Schiff who had made his money in insurance and was most interested in better arts coverage.

Fox was inspired by a paper called *Nashville Scene*. "Two guys had taken a shopper newspaper and turned it into an alternative weekly. I thought 'Crap if they can do that in Nashville'—I had lived in Nashville and didn't like the South—'there's got to be a way we can do it in Cincinnati.'"

More than Detroit, Cleveland, or Pittsburgh, Republican-dominated Cincinnati was hurting for a liberal publication. "The *Enquirer* was conservative and the *Post* was sort of middle of the road—it wasn't anywhere near being liberal," says Fox. Fox and Schiff made a good team because Schiff, the money man, wasn't interested in meddling in the paper's political coverage. That was Fox's department.

"I know that first year, we spent hundreds of thousands of dollars and had very few ads," says Fox. "But we got the critical mass going—most of the arts organizations and music clubs backed us right away. Then the restaurants came along as well. It always takes a while for the more established people—the car dealers and banks and retail stores to come around—because this is a hippie newspaper and the word 'fuck' is in there so it's like giving money to devil worshippers." A right-to-life group and an anti-gay marriage group called Citizens for Community values "used to hound us all the time," Fox remembers.

The conservative groups mounted letter-writing campaigns, which got *CityBeat* banned from Kroger grocery stores for a good long while, "but eventually we got back in. There were people who supported us. There's definitely a subculture of musicians and artists and young people who want to live in the city—that was what I always thought—a paper like *CityBeat*, if you were somebody who was different, a musician or artist or gay or a Democrat, there was a newspaper for you. It made you feel like 'Hey, I'm not the only freak in Cincinnati.' It made you feel better, and maybe it made you want to stay in Cincinnati."

Many alternative newspapers don't do political endorsements. But endorsements were the bread and butter of CityBeat. "Our endorsements were pretty much the opposite of what the daily papers' were," says Fox. They were the only paper to endorse Mark Mallory in his 2005 mayoral campaign against a popular city council member. Mallory won, becoming the first elected African-American mayor of Cincinnati. "It was one of those things where I thought, maybe we actually made a difference there," says Fox.

Like *In Pittsburgh*, *CityBeat* also pushed hard for a police citizen review board, in their case after the 2001 riots sparked by the police killing of an unarmed African-American man. "We covered it every week for months and months and months," says Fox. "We were very critical of the police."

In 2012, Fox and Schiff sold *CityBeat* to Southcomm, the Nashville-based owner of *Nashville Scene* and six other alternative weeklies. The 2000s were hard times for alternative newspapers. Craigslist sucked away much of the classified advertising, the shift to online publishing fragmented the market, and larger economic trends didn't cooperate. "We were doing well until the riots and 9/11 hit, then from 2002 through 2008, we were struggling," says Fox. "In 2008, we were doing much better, but then the economy collapsed and we were back down again."

In Pittsburgh, Potter is constantly finding ways to stretch a shrinking budget, while still publishing in print once a week and updating content continuously online.

"It's tough," he says. "My paycheck clears, but the staff is smaller. The paper is absolutely smaller—there's just a lot less space to do stuff. When we had much larger papers, it was possible to cover all the bases in terms of the hard news you wanted to cover and the bands people wanted to hear about, and also do a three- or four-thousand word story on what was up with the mayor's fucked-up downtown redevelopment strategy. And we're not in that position now. We had an ability, that I think we lack now, to set an agenda for ourselves say, 'as a paper we're mission-driven in this, that and the other.'"

To cut costs, Potter got rid of all the paper's columns ("that function of alt-weeklies has gone by the wayside," he says), figuring money would be better spent on reported pieces—like an exposé on the Pittsburgh-based for-profit college company Education Management Company, a billion-dollar firm that was posting huge revenues largely comprised of government-funded student loans.

Potter doesn't see alt weeklies as central to the identity of a city or region as they were in the 1980s and '90s. "I think that existential mission as I originally encountered it, there are other places you can find that too.

"There are times when you have to do a story about artisanal ice cubes—I'm not making this up—and I'm thinking, 'This is not what I signed up for. I don't want to pay $14 for a goddamn cocktail.'

"I don't know where this ends up. I don't know where this paper is in five years. I don't think anybody knows where their paper is in five years. I'm just going to play out this dream as best I can, and just try to find stories and people getting pushed around. If it all comes to an end today, I would like to leave something behind besides … yet another cutting-edge, paradigm-shifting cocktail bar. I'd like it to be about something more than that."

BELT'S QUICK GUIDE TO ALT-WEEKLY HISTORY

Paper	*Fifth Estate*	*Scene*
City	Detroit	Cleveland
Year Founded	1966	1970
Founded How	By a 17-yr-old in his parents' basement	By a gas station owner with a loan from his dad
One-Word Description	Badass	Muscular
Big Stories	Coverage of the Detroit riots in 1967	"Comrades in Crime," an expose on an East Side computer smuggling ring
Most Affirming Reader Response	National Guardsmen threw hand grenade through their office window	A 1999 cover story on swingers with racy art drew a torrent of hate mail
Current Status	Same ownership since the beginning	After 15 years of out of town owners, now back in local hands
Relatives (Dead or Alive)	*Creem, Metro Times*	*Alternative Press*

Edition	City Paper	City Beat
Cleveland	Pittsburgh	Cincinnati
1986	1990	1994
"I saw someone with a New York magazine T-shirt. I thought, 'What publication in Cleveland would I want the T-shirt of? None.'"	By a Christmas tree farm and dating hotline magnate, to compete with a paper that wouldn't take dating-hotline ads.	"If Nashville can do this, so can we."
Writerly	Tenacious	Iconoclastic
Roldo Bartimole's columns hammering away at the sin tax for Gateway	Rich Lorde's series on subprime mortgage lending in the early 2000s; for-profit art school investigation	Coverage of police misconduct that culminated in the 2001 riots
Readers sent in money in a last-ditch effort to try and save the paper	City officials yanked the paper off their press release list and then denied that they did it	Letter writing campaign to Kroger by right-to-lifers who didn't want *City Beat* near their produce
Closed and resurrected twice. Lid nailed on the coffin in 1992.	Since 1998, owned by Steel City Media, which also owns classic rock and light FM radio stations. "We have the worst hold music in the world."	Sold in 2012 to a Nashville-based alt-weekly company
Free Times, Buddhist Third Class Junkmail Oracle (published by poet D.A. Levy)	*In Pittsburgh*	*Everybody's News*

Dispatches from the Rust Belt

III. History

Dispatches from the Rust Belt

Train Dreams

Pete Beatty

"Not a great while ago, passing through the gate of dreams, I visited that region of the earth in which lies the famous City of Destruction. It interested me much to learn that by the public spirit of some of the inhabitants a railroad has recently been established between this populous and flourishing town and the Celestial City"

— Nathaniel Hawthorne, "The Celestial Railroad"

T*he Van Sweringen brothers* started out as office boys at a fertilizer company. They ended up, like everyone else, as fertilizer. In the interim, they became very rich, and then went very broke. The brothers were millionaires many times over, but their name never became a metonym for wealth, like Croesus, Fugger, Carnegie, or Rockefeller.

The brothers—universally referred to as just "the Vans"—built the type of pile that outlasts a human lifespan. This level of wealth typically lingers on in the names of parks, museum wings, scholarships, or campus building, reminding the living world of just how much money O.P. and M.J. earned in their 50-odd years of existence. But the Van Sweringens have no such legacy.

The Vans hammered Cleveland into a new shape on the anvil of their ambition. They built one of the most affluent suburban communities in the world, Shaker Heights, from nothing, articulating a romantic, upmarket version of the American dream, and sold that dream to an upper middle class desperate to stratify itself from the soiled reality of Cleveland. They linked their utopian community to booming, dirty downtown Cleveland with rapid transit. They built Terminal Tower—a gleaming city-within-a-city meant to vault Cleveland into the front rank of American metropolises. And they built a massive train station underneath their skyscraper, and displaced thousands to do so. They remade the country, too. From a rattling six-mile streetcar line, the Vans improbably assembled a 20,000-mile railroad empire that spanned the continent.

By 1930, the year their Terminal Tower had its gala grand opening in downtown Cleveland, brothers Mantis James and Oris Paxton Van Sweringen shared a personal fortune of about $120 million ($1.6 billion in 2013 dollars), and controlled a railroad and real estate empire worth nearly $3 billion (which translates to $40 billion today).

They remade Cleveland and they remade themselves into lords of commerce on a national scale. But it wasn't enough to merit a high school or a road named after them. Their name is vanished from the earth, save for their shared plot in Lake View Cemetery.

Why have they been forgotten? Partially because the brothers were fixated on avoiding publicity, even as their business holdings grew and grew. They shunned interviewers and photographers. A massive celebratory luncheon for thousands of VIPs marked the official opening of the Terminal Tower, but O.P. and M.J. stayed at home and listened on the radio. Their intense modesty had an eccentric edge. Both brothers were lifelong bachelors, and occupied twin beds in a single room of their 54-room mansion.

They have also vanished because their empire vanished; in fact, their kingdom crumbled before their eyes. Their businesses, a warren of interlocking directorates and paper holding companies, imploded in the Great Depression. The brothers—previously praised as the greatest of Cleveland's self-made men—were denounced as crooks, fleecers of the public trust, examples of the financial recklessness that had brought about economic cataclysm.

Just a few short years after the Terminal Tower opened, the brothers were broke. The Vans were not the only business giants to lose it all, but they have no rivals for how far and how fast they fell.

§

Gerret van Sweringen sailed from Holland and arrived in the Delaware colony in 1657. He was the first in a dignified succession of sturdy, well-to-do Van Sweringens—landowners, gentleman farmers, pillars of various communities. For close to two centuries, the Van Sweringens thrived.

James Sweringen (the *tussenvoegsel* disappeared somewhere between 1657 and Jim's adulthood) was the first Sweringen to find America less than hospitable.

He served in the Union Army in the Civil War, and was seriously wounded at the battle of Spotsylvania Court House in 1864. His injuries would always hinder him. He bounced from job to job and place to place with his wife, Jennie. He worked in the oil fields of Pennsylvania for a time, but by 1879, he was working on a farm in Chippewa Township, near Wooster, Ohio. There and then his fifth child (the fourth to survive infancy) was born, with the unusual name of Oris Paxton Sweringen. Two years later, the family had relocated to Rogue's Hollow, not far away. A sixth child, and third son, was born in the summer of 1881. He was dubbed Mantis James. No definite explanation for the strange names was ever recorded—the other Sweringen siblings bear common names.

From the beginning, the two younger brothers were inseparable. Oris was the shorter of the two, with dark hair. He was slow and thoughtful. Mantis was blond, sprightly, logical, and in the words of one biographer, "somewhat intense." They lost their mother early—Jennie succumbed to tuberculosis in 1886. Not long after, the family drifted to Geneva, Ohio, and eventually to Cleveland. Jim was an alcoholic by then, and no longer much for working. He looked to his five children to keep the family in their home near E. 105th Street and Cedar Avenue, in what was then a sparsely settled fringe of Cleveland, and is now an asphalt prairie of hospital-complex parking lots.

Oris and Mantis dropped out of school after 8th grade. Their business careers got off to very modest starts: newspaper routes, hauling groceries, running errands, tending cattle, lighting streetlamps. Eventually, oldest sibling Herbert drafted his brothers into clerkships at the

Bradley Fertilizer Company, on salaries of $15 a week.

Fertilizer wasn't their calling, though. Herbert and Oris soon started a short-lived stone dealership. Mantis launched a dairy delivery. Then O.P. and M.J.—they went by their initials professionally, although they called each other by their given names—teamed up to launch a cartage company. They would be inseparable in business thereafter, but the cartage firm didn't last. Neither did a subsequent bicycle shop.

Nothing stuck—in part because O.P. was pursuing a vision. He would enter the world of real estate at the age of 21, he had decided. And so he did. The Sweringen empire began very modestly. O.P. negotiated an option to sell a house on the East Side of Cleveland. This entailed listing a house that he didn't yet own, but would pay for out of the proceeds of the eventual sale. The leveraged buyout, wobbly financed, was a Sweringen trademark from the very beginning. The brothers cleared $100 in the deal. They were in the game.

Their momentum didn't last long. They bought a number of lots in the emerging west side suburb of Lakewood, but their investment was foreclosed upon. The reasons for the foreclosure are lost to time, but the judgment discouraged the Vans from doing business under their own names for two years. They bought and sold under the names of their sisters for a time. When they re-emerged, the Sweringens had become the Van Sweringens once more. Some biographers have speculated that this was to distance themselves from the Lakewood foreclosure; perhaps it was just a mild affectation.

§

In the first decade of the 20th century, Cleveland was booming. The lost decade of the 1890s was over, and the city's industrial heart was pumping furiously. The boom was making many Clevelanders rich, but it was also crowding them. The city's population had rocketed from roughly 92,000 in 1870 to 380,000 in 1900; it would double again by 1920.

The business and residential center of the city was perched on a narrow lakefront wedge, with the heavy industry of the Cuyahoga Valley to the south and Lake Erie to the north. Crossing the river to Ohio City to the west meant navigating the steep walls of the valley and waiting through traffic gnarled by the constant interruption of ships on the river. The opening of the Superior Viaduct in 1878 had made westward expansion more feasible. But the mighty viaduct still had to swing its drawbridge center open multiple times a day for ships to pass on the river. The first high bridge across the river would not open until 1917.

The West Side would do for immigrants and the laboring classes—they had no choice but to accept a slow streetcar ride home. But the well-to-do sorely needed an escape from the increasingly busy, dirty, and overcrowded center. Dirty is no exaggeration; even as late as the 1940s, it was estimated that the average Cleveland resident inhaled as much as five pounds of soot per year. The industry that was making some Clevelanders rich belched storms of smoke into the air, in addition to hundreds of trains and thousands of chimneys.

With western suburbs still lacking in quality, and water to both north and south, the east was the only feasible outlet for Cleveland's bourgeoisie. After the Civil War, the extremely swell had built a strip of small castles along Euclid Avenue. This district became famous beyond Cleveland for its grandeur. But rapid growth thwarted even the ultra-rich; Millionaire's Row wasn't safe from the sprawl of downtown. Regular workaday rich folks wanted to distance themselves from the overly vibrant city center, without the burden of a lengthy commute.

§

The land that would become Shaker Village was first surveyed in 1796, and "found to be well stocked with timber, grapevines, howling wolves, Indians, bees, and honey," according to historian Ian Haberman. Very little of note happened on the land until 1822, when the North Union Society of the Millennium Church of United Believers built a colony there. The Shakers, as they were better known, had come into the land when one of their number inherited a section of a Western Reserve land grant.

The Shakers referred to their 1,360-acre spread as "The Valley of God's Pleasure," even though it was actually on a bluff. The valley referenced the stream running through the acreage, which the Shakers dammed for a mill. The Shakers set about waiting for the second coming, farming and making crafts. Their colony prospered for a time. But eventually their policy of celibacy caught up with them, as it always does. Their numbers dwindled, and by 1889 the colony had only a handful of ancients remaining. The Shakers decided to close down their utopia.

The remaining believers sold out for $316,000 to a consortium of businessmen from Buffalo, New York, headed by a man named William Gratwick. The Buffalo syndicate hoped to develop the spread, just six miles from downtown Cleveland. But they had chosen the wrong decade. The stock market cratered in 1893, setting off the worst economic depression in the nation's history to date. Thousands of businesses collapsed, including many banks. Double-digit unemployment was pervasive; in some larger cities, the unemployed rolls swelled to 33 percent of eligible workers. It was not a good decade to be developing suburbia.

The Shaker lands sat fallow for more than a decade, the farms and outbuildings gently decaying. In 1905, the Van Sweringen brothers, all of 26 and 24 years old, approached the Gratwick syndicate with a peculiar deal. They wanted options to sell lots, no money down. They'd pay once they sold the land, out of the proceeds. For the landowner, this doesn't seem like much of a bargain. But the Buffalonians were already worried about their investment. They had paid $316,000 in 1889. But in 1900, the land was appraised for just $240,000.

Permitting two twenty-somethings to flip a few homesteads likely seemed better than sitting around watching the investment sink farther underwater. The Vans took 30-day options on small plots. Their deal with the Buffalo group stipulated that if the brothers successfully sold their first option, they would receive a 60-day option on twice as much land. Each successive deal included the same clause. The brothers made good on their options repeatedly.

§

Even as the Vans sold their modest options on the Shaker land, a master plan was coalescing in their minds. With ambitious planning and careful executions, the brothers would build the utopia that those three hundred Shakers had sought in vain. Where the old Shakers had sat around waiting for Jesus and making furniture, O.P. and M.J. would build up a garden city, a place where the white-collar workers of Cleveland could build a "forever home." In the words of their own marketing pamphlet, their new model suburb would be "a secure haven for the home-harried; for those ruthlessly ousted from the paths of the City's progress; for those wishing to establish homes which shall memorialize them for generations to come."

Shaker Village, as the Vans called it, would have everything a suburb could possibly need. There would be stately homes built to splendid and harmonious styles, fine schools, country clubs, and designated retail districts, all "conspicuously free from the throat ailments so prevalent on the City levels," promotional material touted. Curved streets would create a bucolic environment, and allow for larger lots and more space between houses. There would be a salubrious mix of mansions and slightly more modest—but still very luxe—homes.

The Vans were no longer interested in flipping real estate for a quick profit. They intended to develop Shaker Village from the sewers on up to the eaves of each home. They would sell a complete package, and every last detail of construction and architecture would be governed by restrictive covenants between buyers and the Van Sweringen Company. If they haphazardly built their new village, would it not soon be swallowed by Cleveland, a city spreading like a brush fire? "Most communities just happen; the best are always planned," announced one article of Van Sweringen propaganda. Another pamphlet crowed that Shaker Village would be "large enough to be self-contained and self-sufficient. No matter what changes time may bring around it, no matter what waves of commercialism may beat upon its border, Shaker Village is secure ... protected for all time."

The new forever-suburb was to be divided into nine ready-made neighborhoods, each with a primary school. Within and across the neighborhoods, the lots were to be divided into zones, with each zone earmarked for a home of a different price tier. The streets were given stodgy-sounding English names. As Shaker Village was built up, some critics mocked its affected hauteur, and dubbed it a "bastion of high-level Babbitry" in the mid-1920s. But the affectation worked—in part because it was deathly earnest. The Vans spared no detail in turning Shaker Village into a model suburb. The Shaker mill ponds were joined by additional artificial lakes. Park land was set aside, never to be developed. More acreage was earmarked for private education. Shaker is still today the home of three elite private schools, Hathaway Brown, the

University School, and the Laurel School.

But one all-important piece of their ten-year plan was not yet secure. Their suburban promised land could not be realized without a transit connection to Cleveland. As their marketing arm mused in yet another piece of persuasive advertising, "whenever and wherever a railroad is built it upturns seeds which immediately spring to life as home communities. It is an interesting reversal of this universal article for a new home community to grow a railroad as part of its development." But that was precisely what the brothers planned. After all, without convenient, comfortable transportation, the burghers of Cleveland would never reach the celestial city the Vans had built for them.

§

O.P. and M.J. approached the Cleveland Electric Railway as early as 1906 with a deal. They wanted the railway to extend a streetcar branch out deep into the Shaker development. In exchange for a car line, the brothers would gift the needed land to the transit concern, and cover the interest on construction costs for five years.

The railway declined the offer, but a streetcar connection to the edge of the Vans' development was built. The scattering of rich pioneers who had scaled the heights already were happy enough to have some way into town, and for their gardeners and maids to be able to get to work.

But the streetcar would not suffice. O.P. and M.J. knew that Shaker Village needed a fast connection to downtown. Streetcar service took three-quarters of an hour or more to reach Public Square. But a car line, or better yet, an electric train, running on its own right-of-way, free from surface traffic, could cover the six miles from Shaker to the heart of downtown in a quarter-hour. But where could they find that right-of-way?

The Vans quietly assembled parcels of land along Kingsbury Run, a watershed running down to the Cuyahoga from the heights to the east. Kingsbury Run wasn't much to look at; O.P. himself described it as "a tin can disposal plant." The area sprouted shantytowns during the recurring economic crises of the early 20th century. Later on, it would be the site of the notorious and still-unsolved Torso Murders.

But the Vans saw something in Kingsbury Run: the hollow provided a natural runway for a rapid transit link between their Shaker Village and the downtown offices of prospective white-collar homeowners. So they bought parcels of land where they could, even as their ten-year plan was just getting underway. But they were still far from a clear right-of-way that would allow streetcars or trains to quickly reach downtown.

§

Billion-dollar fortunes don't happen without luck. And in 1911, a large measure of luck found the Vans. They had bought a 25-acre farm in what is now Pepper Pike the year before, to the east of the Shaker lands (eventually the brothers would own a total of 4,000 acres of the eastside suburbs). Across the road from their property was a spread owned by the widow of a lately deceased railroad man. O.P. called upon the widow, who put him in touch with her brother, who spoke for her in business matters.

The widow's brother was Alfred Holland Smith, a vice president of the New York Central Railroad, soon to become the president of the massive Central. In the course of making one modest real estate transaction, Smith and O.P. made a connection that would alter both of their fates profoundly.

The Central moved more rail traffic—freight and passenger— through Cleveland than any other line. Accordingly it was suffering badly from Cleveland's rotten railroad facilities. The outdated Union Depot station and the lakefront tracks were hopelessly snarled. The Central had recently built a short freight bypass that cut to the south of the congested center, but they needed both a new freight yard and a convenient location for that yard.

Kingsbury Run could provide both. Smith didn't waste much time in seeing what partnership he could make with the two brothers. In August 1913, the freshly incorporated Cleveland & Youngstown Railroad began construction on a four-track railroad stretching from E. 34th Street to E. 91st. Smith's Central quietly paid the bills, although the tight-lipped Vans would neither confirm nor deny that particular point. The New York Central would build a freight depot in Kingsbury Run, and would use two of the four tracks. The other half would belong to the Vans.

§

With more discreet assistance from the New York Central, the Shaker Heights Rapid commenced service in April 1920. The line cost $8 million to build. Its electric cars ran express from the heights down to E. 34th Street, finishing the final mile and a half to Public Square on city streetcar tracks. The journey took 27 minutes. Eventually the time would be trimmed to just 12 minutes.

A commemorative brochure handed out on the first day of Rapid service stressed the vision the Vans had now completed: "Think what it will mean to Cleveland business people to have protected homes where there is no possibility of invasion by unwelcome buildings of any sort; where they can depend on this protection as long as they live; where the inevitable growth and spread of a 'million city' cannot alter or affect the simple conditions under which their homes are established."

With the rapid transit link secure, a decade of planning paid out spectacularly. The Vans were rich. The Shaker land had been appraised at roughly a quarter million dollars in 1900. A decade later, it was worth $2.5 million. By 1920, the former Valley of God's Pleasure was valued at $11.8 million. A mere three years after that staggering leap, Shaker Village was worth $29.3 million in 1923. From a population of 1,600 in 1920, Shaker would be home to 18,000 by the end of that roaring decade.

And in dabbling in transportation, the brothers had stumbled— or were gently pushed—into a new line of business. Railroading would transform the Vans from local operators to titans of business, and it would also destroy them.

Fun Town: Chicago's Last Amusement Park

Jake Austen

Marcie Hill was seven years old when the fun died. In 1982, Fun Town, the last amusement park within Chicago's city limits, ended its 32-year run of thrilling South Side children. For Hill, warm memories of spending time with her mother in a dynamic communal space in her own neighborhood linger every time she passes the strip malls that now occupy the real estate at 95th Street between Stony Island and Jeffrey Boulevard.

Upon realizing her memories were murky (she recalls the pride of being able to go on small-scale rides by herself, but not the exact rides), Hill began researching the park for *Shorty*, her South Side-themed blog. Though her search turned up a treasure trove of information about Riverview, the massive North Side amusement park that enchanted Chicago from 1904 through 1967, there was virtually nothing about Fun Town. One of the only mentions of the park in the *Chicago Tribune* was a tiny obituary of the park's founder with wildly inaccurate information, and the Newberry Library's *Encyclopedia of Chicago* documents numerous amusement parks, but omits her favorite one.

"As relevant as Fun Town was to my people, there should have been more press and more information available," Hill laments. "This was an important part of Chicago history and black history. To see no record of it ... it feels like people just don't value the South Side."

It's not too surprising that a modest eight-acre park, which at its peak had a couple of dozen rides, has been given history's cold shoulder. One of Chicago's defining achievements was hosting the grandest carnival imaginable, the 1893 World's Fair (followed forty years later by its modernist sequel). And Riverview *was* spectacular: 140 acres filled with over a hundred attractions, including the massive Fireball rollercoaster, and a full sideshow. Yet it's understandable that South Siders who held Fun Town dear, and who have come to expect patterns of second-class treatment, feel slighted every few years when yet another PBS special casts a nostalgic eye upon Riverview's tattooed ladies and world-class coasters.

Despite its size Fun Town *was* important. At its birth it represented the baby boomers' early influence on American amusements. In the 1960s when radical shifts in the racial demographics of the South Side took place, it peacefully transitioned from a majority white park to a majority black park while recreation spots around the city and the country were experiencing riots and protests. And during the seventies, thanks to black management, a funky jingle, and doors opened by Riverview's doors shutting, it became a source of community pride in the heart of the black pride era. By ignoring the action that took place at 1711 E. 95th Street, history has been missing out on some serious fun.

§

In 1950 Harold "Cookoo" Greenwald, a South Shore entrepreneur, built the park, originally called Kiddy Town, from the ground up. Prior to that endeavor, Greenwald (who lettered in football at University of Michigan in 1926 and was recruited by the NFL's Chicago Cardinals, but did not make the team), managed the Lion's Club downtown, worked as a store detective at Goldblatt's, and owned taverns. His son, Ted Greenwald, doesn't recall what motivated his father to go into the amusement park industry, but at that time "kiddie" parks (with smaller, tamer rides than standard amusement parks) were a burgeoning business thanks to the postwar baby boom. Though the idea was not new (Kiddieland in Melrose Park, a northwest Chicago suburb, opened in 1929), in the fifties these parks rapidly proliferated. A 1953 newspaper ad (refuting a rumor about deadly rattlesnake attacks at local parks) listed 14

Chicagoland members of the Kiddie Park Operators' Association.

In the 1950s the park established many of the features it would proudly host for most of its run, including pony rides, go karts, trampolines, a small roller coaster, mini golf, and merry-go-rounds (including the Kiddie Tank Ride, with World War II-era tanks in place of horses). Though tiny compared to Riverview, for the tiny ones in the region it was paradise.

"The best part of my life was growing up on the South Side," recalls Dianne White, who lived in South Shore in the fifties and sixties. "Kiddy Town was so exciting, right off of a busy street, just this colorful place in the heart of the South Side. If we got good grades, we were allowed to go. It was a place we really considered to be our own. Riverview was for the North Side, but this was close to our house."

At the time the demographics of the park clientele reflected the population of the area, which had many Jewish and Greek Orthodox families (the Nation of Islam's Mosque Maryam on Stony Island was originally a Greek Orthodox church). Some Hispanic and black families visited the park, but the customers were overwhelmingly white.

Sometime after Greenwald's 1963 death, Alan Carvell Jr. and his wife June Marie Carvell took over park ownership. They also owned the Rainbo ice skating rink on the North Side (later the Rainbo roller rink), which briefly doubled as the Kinetic Playground in the 1960s, a rock club that hosted Jimi Hendrix, Led Zeppelin, and the Who.

Around 1968, presumably in reaction to the closing of Riverview, Kiddy Town acquired a Wild Mouse roller coaster, a Rock-O-Plane ride, and other attractions aimed at older kids and teens. The name was changed to Fun Town (sometimes written as Funtown), and the park's phone book display ad now boasted a whopping 18 rides (to go along with go karts, batting cages, and a "swinging gym"). The patrons, by then predominantly black, enjoyed a park that was often bustling, but never overcrowded. There were rarely long lines to board the Moon Rocket, take a spin on the Trabant, or go down the Astro Slide. And the prices were fair, with no admission charge, cheap ride tickets, half price coupons from Jewel supermarket, and (according to a 1971 ad) all-day ride passes on special days for $2.

The park's chain of ownership has been difficult to verify, especially in the later years when it may have changed hands several times, and ownership/management groups may have been involved. The park leased out various sections, receiving rent and a percentage of receipts, so the arcade, for example, had a separate owner. Keith McDonald, who worked at the park from 1973 to 1975 stocking the food stands with cotton candy, corndogs, and sno-cone fixings, told me he believed several police officers, including Ira Harris, were park owners, but that does not appear to be the case, though Harris was in upper management, and did most of the hiring. David Dines, a ride operator and park marshal from 1975 to 1982 believes the Carvells maintained ownership until 1977. He attributes the park's decline to the 1977 takeover (either as owners or managers) by Jack Thompson Shows, an out of town interest that ran the park like a low-grade travelling carnival. After several years of bad management, he says, a well-intentioned man named Bob Johnson became the final owner, renaming it Big "J" Funtown, before the park gave its last ride in 1982.

§

Perhaps contributing to Fun Town's low historical profile was summer after summer of uneventful amusements. Though Riverview's long tenure saw several ride-related deaths, and 72 riders injured in a 1937 roller coaster accident, no such excitement occurred on the South Side. Ted Greenwald, who worked part time at his father's park as a ride operator ("he promised I would get to run the Shetland pony concession, but I never got it,") doesn't recall any serious accidents in the fifties, and the only lawsuit he remembers involved a child being slightly bruised after falling off a train ride. Bob Gas, whose father was the maintenance manager from 1965 until 1982, and whose mother worked in the kitchen (Bob worked concessions) is pretty sure there were no serious injuries or deaths (not even from snake attacks) during his years there. "My Dad took great pride in making sure that every nut and bolt was checked and double tightened, especially on the larger rides."

The countless kids protected by Mr. Gas's busy wrench included many groups of underprivileged children brought on trips by a variety of organizations. The *Chicago Defender* newspaper documented a 1965 free day for a thousand West Side kids sponsored by the Chicago Commission of Youth Welfare and the Chicago Committee on Urban Opportunity. The Englewood Urban Progress Center brought seven hundred kids to the park in 1970. The *Defender* announced the 21st Police District-sponsored Fun Day bringing in three thousand kids in 1971. Jesse Jackson's Operation Push also hosted events, and Mayor Richard J. Daley bussed in kids from city day camps.

Like many South Siders, Keith McDonald's childhood visits to Riverview made deep impressions, but ultimately he felt more of an affinity to the park in his backyard. "On the South Side you didn't see people outside of your ethnic group, but at Riverview you saw everybody," he remembers. "It was so big, and they had the guy with the bubble eyes and the lady with the beard...but Fun Town was in my neighborhood. Seeing excitement on familiar faces, hearing James Brown music at the batting cages, having a place for all the teenagers to hang out...we had cotton candy back then, we didn't have shootings."

§

Unlike legendary parks like Riverview and Brooklyn's Coney Island, Fun Town is rarely cited as a cultural reference (Chicago rapper Common makes a brief mention in his nostalgic 1994 song "Nuthin' To Do" and one book from Arcadia Publishing has a photo from the 1950s mislabeled as "Kiddyland"). However, a different Funtown looms large in American culture. In Dr. Martin Luther King's powerful 1963 "Letter from Birmingham Jail," the Civil Rights leader recalls his daughter's excitement at seeing a TV commercial for a local amusement park, followed by "tears welling up in her eyes when she is told that Funtown is closed to colored children." That story (most recently revived in Martin Luther King III's 2013 children's book, *My Daddy, Martin Luther King, Jr.*) was about an Atlanta park with a far different history than Chicago's Fun Town (despite both operating a Wild Mouse coaster). But the story does bring up two subjects that make Chicago's Fun Town so important to South Siders: promotions and racial politics.

In contrast to Atlanta's park, Fun Town in Chicago didn't advertise on television (though in the 50s when TV personalities like Two Ton Baker made park appearances, their fee also paid for an announcement of the event on their show). But mention Fun Town to nearly any

Chicagoan who listened to black local radio in the 1970s and they likely will respond in song, wistfully recalling the popular jingle, "Fun Town, Fun Town for the kids and you/ 95th and Stony Island Av-e-*nue*...*Fun Town!*" Though the park also advertised itself with a small fire truck with "Fun Town" painted on the door (which would pick up kids for birthday parties), by far their most successful promotional activity in the seventies was placing this infectious jingle on Chicago black radio stations WVON, WJPC, and WMPP (the East Chicago Heights station that also served Gary, Indiana's R&B needs). Though Fun Town's radio commercials changed over the years (they sometimes featured mascot Suzy Funtown, a character resembling Stephanie Mills' Dorothy from "The Wiz," who also made live park appearances), the joyous jingle remained the same.

The song was the handiwork of Richard Pegue, an iconic figure in Chicago radio. As a teen in the late fifties, like many of his peers, he had a high school vocal group. But Pegue didn't just want his songs played on the radio, he wanted to understand every aspect of radio and music production. The teen tape machine tinkerer began working behind the scenes writing, producing, and engineering music, as well as deejaying neighborhood parties. He eventually gained fame as one of the "Good Guys," the legendary disc jockeys at WVON ("The Voice of the Negro," the influential station owned by the Chess Brothers). Less prominent was his music production career, but as Numero Group's 2011 compilation of his productions argues, Pegue was a special talent. In a town famed for sweet harmonies, he arranged and recorded some of the sweetest, and his compositions and arrangements were groovy, whimsical, and memorable.

But after his failure to produce a hit record by the early 70s, his record producing dreams were put on the back shelf. Pegue, however, never stopped recording. He had a knack for jingle writing and over the years he produced memorable local spots for North Grand Auto Parts, Wallace's Catfish Corner (featuring soulman Otis Clay on vocals), and his most enduring promotion, the Moo and Oink meat warehouse ads that he continued to record weekly in his analog home studio until he passed away in 2009. "His commercials weren't slapped together," recalls disc jockey PJ Willis, a Pegue protégé who sometimes helped on the spots. "He had a personal touch you don't usually hear in commercial work."

That was the touch he applied to his great 1970 Fun Town jingle, the recording that started his alternate career. "I was working at WVON," Pegue told Chicago soul historian Bob Abrahamian in a 2009 interview, "and one of the salesmen had an account for an amusement park...I heard their commercials and they were rather blasé. So I struck up an association with the people who ran the park, and they said they need something, and I said I need something...money!" Pegue's first jingle borrowed a backing track from a 1969 studio instrumental he produced called "For Brothers Only" by the group The Brothers & Sisters, though the vocal act has little to do on the lyric-free song (a serial recycler, in 1981 Pegue would add jingle bells to the track and use it again for a radio station Christmas single). After adding professional singers emoting the catchy couplet, Pegue's production was solid but needed something extra to appeal to the Fun Town crowd.

Eight year-old Lorenzo Modeste and his ten year-old sister Lisa Ramirez were brought by their mother, a friend of Pegue's, to the WVON studios. They put on headphones, got behind the microphone and did the spoken intro ("Hey mama, hey daddy, let's go to Fun Town...") and then sang along with the pre-recorded vocal tracks. Pegue paid their mother enough to buy the children a dresser for their bedroom, but the real compensation came when the song hit the WVON airwaves less than a week later. "Within a few days," Modeste (now a dentist in Virginia) recalls, "we became instant celebrities." The song remained on the air until he graduated high school. In addition, the "Fun Town Kids" received free ride tickets for the rest of their childhoods.

The popularity of the jingle was proven on the days Lisa and Lorenzo mounted the Funtown Stage (not to be confused with the short-lived, Pegue-programmed Funtown Disco Stage, a 35-foot flatbed trailer precariously parked on the inclined concrete of the former batting cages). The siblings sang along to their "hit" as the crowd cheered the youngsters, thrilled to see the radio stars in the flesh. (Pegue fans should note that Lisa was also the juvenile voice declaring, "*You got a funny name*," at the start of each of his radio shows)

§

Though that jingle remains the most memorable facet of Fun Town, the park's real legacy may be the way it survived and thrived during the seventies when urban amusement parks were disappearing. Specifically, Fun Town, unlike so many amusement parks around the country, did not disappear because a black populace took over the neighborhood. Instead it flourished, becoming a point of pride for teens holding down their first jobs, parents appreciating affordable family entertainment, and kids able to experience something special without leaving their corner of the city. In an era when an ethos of self-sufficiency was profoundly important to the black community, Fun Town was something South Siders felt belonged to them.

That narrative is unique, according to University of Buffalo SUNY professor Victoria Wolcott, author of *Race, Riots, and Roller Coasters*. As racial populations shifted in the 20th Century, urban recreational facilities wary of desegregation were often sites of violence and protests. Midwest unrest ensued in Cleveland (where a Euclid Beach security guard shot an off-duty black police officer during a desegregation protest), in Cincinnati (where protestors spent nine years picketing, blocking gates, and going to jail to fully integrate their Coney Island amusement park), and 4.5 miles from Fun Town at Rainbow Beach, the site of a 1961 "wade in" demonstration, in which black and white swimmers entered the water together, and were subsequently attacked by white youth gangs throwing rocks. At Riverview Park, black patrons were admitted, but were likely uncomfortable with the "Dunk the Nigger" dunk tank attraction on the midway (later re-named "The African Dip," and ultimately shut down after NAACP protests in the late 1950s). Many parks (including Atlanta's Funtown) closed rather than dealing with integration. According to Wolcott, the massive suburban parks that replaced them used high entrance fees (as opposed to cheap per-ride tickets) to filter out undesired populaces.

Fun Town avoided these tensions, in part because white flight was so rapid in the area. In 1968 there was only one black girl in Dianne White's eighth grade class but by 1970 hers was one of only three remaining white families in the neighborhood. The amusement park's demographic shift followed suit. The park may have also avoided some of the tensions that plagued other sites because it catered only to small children during much of the fifties and sixties, the influx of "threatening" black teens coming only after the 1968 shift to the Fun

Town name, when white families were already leaving the area. One disturbing urban myth that plagued Riverview claimed it was a space for black teenagers to rape white girls.

In contrast, instead of damning black youth with dangerous stereotypes, Fun Town presented them with models of success, and not only with visiting celebrities like Pegue, fellow Good Guy Herb Kent, and athletes like Ernie Banks. Because Fun Town was closed in the winter, and only operated weekends when school was in session, the black managers and concession owners were moonlighting at the park, and many had successful outside careers. Leo Ammons, who owned the carnival games, also had his own construction company. And Ira Harris was one of the more prominent African-American police officers in Chicago. He would go on to be president of NOBLE, the National Organization of Black Law Enforcement Executives, and also served as Chief of Police of the Chicago Housing Authority.

Fun Town represented opportunity for many local teens. Terrance Morris, now Operations Director for CAN-TV (Chicago's cable access network), managed carnival games at the park from 1972 through 1976, starting when he was barely a teen. "Working there taught me responsibility, and showed us it was possible to make something of ourselves. A lot of what I do in my job today I learned working at Fun Town."

One anecdote McDonald wistfully recalls says it all for him in terms of what Fun Town meant to the South Side. "One time I had to close and didn't leave until after 11, and while I was waiting for the bus at 95th and Stony a policeman approached and asked to see my ID. But then he saw my red and white Fun Town shirt, and that was ID enough. That shirt was iconic in the neighborhood, if you worked at Fun Town everyone knew you were okay."

§

By the early 80s, Fun Town was not okay. Mismanagement chipped away at the goodwill associated with the park. Increasing poverty in a neighborhood where once everyone could work in the nearby US Steel mill, which laid off half its workers by 1980, led to increased crime.

Gas recalls overnight break-ins which resulted in German shepherd dogs patrolling the park at night. "Sadly," he says "several of them were found dead, some poisoned and some shot." The increasing popularity of the suburban mega-amusement park Great America, which opened in 1976, was the final nail in Fun Town's casket. "There were some nights," David Dines recalls, "where there might have been five customers in the park. It was really sad and hopeless." In 1982 the rides were auctioned, the land sold, and Chicago's last amusement park was no more.

"Places of urban recreation were such important spaces for residents of these communities," Wolcott reflects. "It's sad they no longer exist."

Terrance Morris concurs. "Fun Town did a lot for the neighborhood in terms of giving kids a safe environment. It was a meeting place, not a lot of riffraff hanging around. If there were something like that today maybe we wouldn't have so much of this violence."

Sing It, Cleveland

Daniel Goldmark

N*ot long after I moved to Cleveland in 2005,* I started researching the city's music history. I discovered dozens of songwriters who created music about life in Cleveland during the early 1900s. Most of these songs were printed as sheet music by now-defunct Cleveland music publishers.

I was delighted. My research and my writing center on the history of popular music, in particular on how people experience songs—whether as a piece of highly decorated paper you could buy in a music shop, as background music heard in cartoons or films, or featured as a performance in a Hollywood musical (to name just a few options).

So I kept—and keep—looking for more evidence of Cleveland's popular music history. I find sheet music all around town: at garage sales, antique shops, library book sales, and when friends of friends give me a call. Hardly a week goes by before I discover something previously unknown. That's the fun of my work and my hobby—I'll probably never see the end of it.

Here are a select few that stand out from what I've found in seven years of digging.

Yes, We Got It, No Hot Dogs (1924)

This song with a very unusual title is a great example of a regional hit, one that never moved beyond the boundaries of the greater Cleveland area. In 1923 the entire country was grinning—or groaning—to the strains of the latest novelty song, "Yes! We Have No Bananas!" The banana song came from the 1922 revue *Make it Snappy* starring the Broadway performer (and later radio, film, and television star) Eddie Cantor. The song and the expression was a pop culture phenomenon, showing up in every imaginable context. Like other pop phenomena, however, the craze wore thin very quickly; a song bemoaning the phrase and its music was published the very same year as the original, titled "I've Got the Yes! We Have No Bananas Blues." This hot dog song, written by Herman Hummel, a prolific Cleveland-based songwriter and arranger, was a featured dance tune at Luna Park in the summer of 1925.

Ideal Home

What better way to sell a home in turn-of-the-century Cleveland than by providing a song that lets the buyer imagine himself singing at the piano, gathered in the secure bosom of a loving family?

The back cover of "The Ideal Home" includes a lengthy sales pitch for the new Crown Point Subdivision, situated "on Noble Road, between Euclid Avenue and Mayfield Road, destined to be another East 105th Street." The price? "$800 to $1000."

The song's composer, Louis Rich, was a Cleveland-born songwriter and bandleader who graduated from East High and wrote several songs-on-demand for Cleveland functions or businesses, including theme songs for the Cleveland Automobile Show in 1915 and another for the Euclid Ave. Opera House (in 1908).

I found this sheet in an antique store on Mayfield Road not far from the area described in the sheet's ad copy; my guess is that someone nearby sold or donated the contents of their piano bench (or, more likely, a box in their attic) to the shop, which would explain why it was so close to its point of origin. The idealist in me imagines a copy of this sheet left as a welcome gift on the fireplace mantle of each new home in the Crown Point Subdivision.

On the Sands

Clevelanders had a wide variety of public beaches, amusement parks, and other forms of diversion to choose from in the early 1900s, and most offered live music by local bands or orchestras for the park-goer. While famous places like Euclid Beach Park and Luna Park attracted thousands, public beaches were also very popular.

Gordon Park opened in 1893; people could fish, swim, boat and use the bathhouse, which is prominently pictured on the sheet music cover. The song's composer, Calvin D. Paxson, best known in Cleveland as a car dealer and owner of Paxson Motors, was an aspiring songwriter who penned quite a few songs, including several extolling the automobile he sold, the Jackson, whose catchphrase was "No Hill Too Steep, No Sand Too Deep."

Adelbert Two-Step

Adelbert Hall was constructed in 1881 as the first building of the newly relocated (from Hudson to Cleveland) Western Reserve University. The song's composer was James D. "Jimmy" Johnston (c.1871-1933). While it's unclear if Johnson went to Western Reserve, he certainly had a propensity for college songs; an article in the *Plain Dealer* from the same year as "Adelbert Two-Step" indicates that he also wrote a "University Two-Step" and "Case Grand March" (neither of which I've ever seen); he also wrote "Yale Varsity" for Cleveland music publisher (and instrument maker) H.N. White in 1901. Johnston was the first principle viola for the Cleveland Orchestra (in 1918) and a member of the Cecilian String Quartet and Philharmonic String Quartet. He also had his own group, the Johnston Society Orchestra, which played in ballrooms and homes throughout Cleveland until his untimely death in his early 60s from a heart attack, suffered while watching a boxing match at the Cleveland Athletic Club.

What dates this song most clearly to 1896 is the dedication to "the Adelbert Mandolin Club." The photograph of the presumed Club showcases a variety of stringed instruments, including a cello, violin, guitars, and mandolins. Instrument clubs were extremely popular for all ages at the turn of the 20th century, and playing the mandolin was all the rage.

My Name Will Always be Chickie

Famous stories ranging from *The Count of Monte Christo* to *The Maltese Falcon* first appeared in serialized installments in magazines and newspapers before being published as standalone books. I've found a craze of sorts for songs inspired by 1920s serials in *The Cleveland News*. Many were by Isobel K. Robertson, a Lakewood resident who authored six songs between 1925 and 1929. While some of these songs didn't get much more than local exposure (read: they never left Cleveland), a few were regional or even national hits, including Robertson's "Nora Lee," and "My Name Will Always Be Chickie," written and popularized by Phil Spitalny, a bandleader who first gained fame in Cleveland with his "all-girl" orchestra and went on to host a radio show heard around the country with the same women's orchestra, called the "Hour of Charm."

Cleveland Industrial Exposition March

At the turn of the 20th century, expositions and world fairs were a very popular way for cities (or countries) to showcase technological advances, trumpet their own ideas of social progress, and create hundreds of jobs and generate revenue. Ohio had many such expos, and songs for them go back at least to the "Cleveland State Fair Waltzes" from the Ohio State Fair in 1852.

The Cleveland Industrial Exposition of 1909 generated at least three songs that I'm aware of, one featuring an original design for the fair by famed artist Ora Coltman, one featuring a statue titled "Spirit of Progress" which was designed by Exposition architect J. Milton Dyer and executed by sculptor Herman Matzen, and the Exposition's "official" publicity image, which highlighted the main exposition building, located where Cleveland City Hall now stands.

Fluffy Ruffle Girls Rag

Here's a perfect example of a Cleveland-published sheet taking on a current pop culture trend. "Fluffy Ruffles" referred to women trying to succeed in the male-dominated workforce. It began as a comic strip in the *New York Herald* in 1906; within a year there were more than a dozen songs published that either had "Fluffy Ruffles" as the title or made reference to "fluffy ruffle" girls. Producer Charles Frohman mounted an entire musical comedy on the theme in 1908, with music by none other than Jerome Kern. Besides the connection to a pop culture trend, the cover's artwork also gives us a vivid snapshot of women's fashion in early 1900s; note that each woman's ensemble varies slightly from the others', not simply in color, but in the hat design, number, size and color of buttons, neckwear, and hairstyle.

Meet Me on the Shores of Old Lake Erie

The Great Lakes Exposition, which ran in the summers of 1936 and 1937, generated more publicity and buzz nationwide than any other fair or event held in Cleveland, including the Industrial Exposition of 1909. Following the mold of world fairs of the past, the Exposition had streets and midways featuring food and commerce from all over the United States and the world, as well as rides, games, and various halls dedicated to history, art, science, and nature.

Live music was a major part of the entertainment, and nothing was more entertaining than producer Billy Rose's song-and-dance-and-swim extravaganza on water, the Billy Rose Aquacade, which only appeared in the 1937 season. The show featured Olympic gold medalists Eleanor Holm and Johnny Weissmuller; both were Hollywood stars, and in 1937 Weissmuller was starring in the very successful *Tarzan* movies.

Most of the music associated with the Exposition came from the Aquacade show and was published by a mainstream New York music publisher. I was thus pleasantly surprised to find a copy of this "Official Song of the Great Lakes Exposition" in a sheet music collection I acquired from a lifelong Clevelander. The song's composer was Walter Logan, who was not only a well-known bandleader on the radio and in concert venues, but also was a one-time head of the Music School Settlement and was among the violinists in the original formation of the Cleveland Orchestra.

Cleveland News March and Two-Step

This piece had and always will have a specific significance for me, in that it is not only an early 20th century song from and about Cleveland—always a plus—but it was (as far as I knew when I found it) the earliest published song by John Stepan Zamecnik. Before setting my sights on Cleveland music, I spent most of my time writing about and watching Hollywood cartoons. Early cartoons—from the late 1920s and through the 1930s—relied a great deal on pop songs and silent movie mood music to fill their soundtracks. Zamecnik was one of the most prolific (and therefore most heard, even though most people have never heard of him) composers of mood music for films, also called photoplay music.

Zamecnik (1872-1953) was a Cleveland native who studied in Prague in his early 20s with Antonin Dvorak before returning to Cleveland, where he was very active as a composer and performer at the turn of the 20th century. He played violin in local orchestras as well as making periodic trips to play in the Pittsburgh Symphony under conductor Victor Herbert; he was the first music director of the Hippodrome Theatre, which opened in late 1907; he was also the staff composer at Sam Fox Publishing. This piece, published by local instrument maker and sometime music publisher H.N. White, commemorates the newly-created *Cleveland News*, which began (out of the merging of three other papers) in the summer of 1905. The song also is one of the dozens of pieces celebrating newspapers in the United States, the most famous example of which was John Philip Sousa's "Washington Post March."

Hurray for Our Baseball Team (1909)

I have several songs about the Indians and even the Browns, but I chose this early song—published in Cleveland—because the cover pictures several major figures from turn of the century baseball. What makes this cover unique is that the men pictured are managers, including many player-managers.

The manager of the Naps, the Cleveland team at the time, was Napoleon Lajoie; he's pictured at top left (his popularity as a player led the team's name to be changed from Bronchos to Naps). Next to LaJoie is Jimmy McAleer, who in 1909 was manager of the St. Louis Browns, but began his career as a player with the Cleveland Spiders and Cleveland Blues. (The stadium pictured is not in Cleveland, by the way; the caption indicates the field is National League Park in Chicago.) While the song's lyrics name almost every major team in the country, the writers figured some smaller teams might want to use the song too: there is a note at the bottom reminding the singer to fill in the "name of your city when singing."

"YES, WE GOT IT, NO HOT DOGS!"
Restaurant
Words by
D. K. Coukoulas
Music by
H. A. Hummel
PUBLISHED BY
COUKOULAS PUB. CO.
CLEVELAND OHIO.

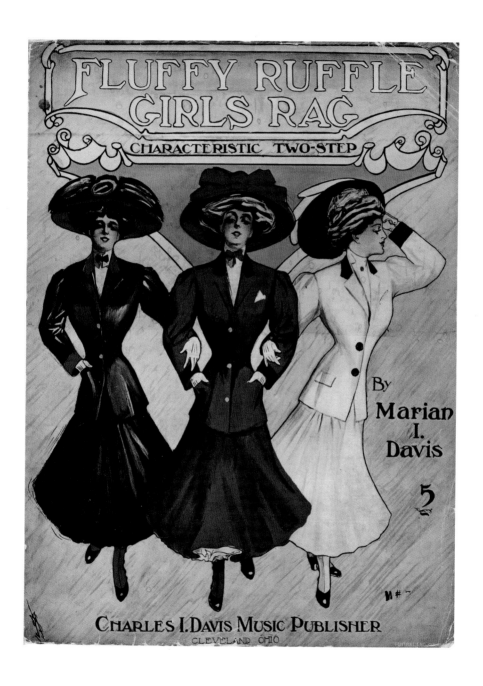

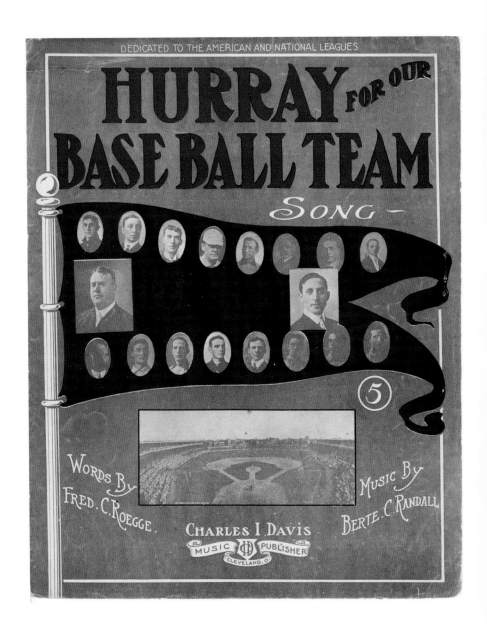

Busing:
A White Girl's Tale

Amanda Shaffer

he Cudell/Edgewater neighborhood where I grew up was a land of immigrant hyphens in the 1970s: Italian-American, Irish-American,
Polish-American and Hungarian-American, just to name a few. Folks
who didn't fit any of these "ethnic categories" had come to Cleveland
from Pennsylvania, West Virginia and Kentucky to find work, and still
called those other places "goin' back home." At the time, everyone I
knew was Catholic; the Indian kids were actually Lakota, and no one
had heard of diversity. Black History Month had just been invented
and Martin Luther King Jr. Day didn't exist yet. It's easy to forget how
different life was. Once upon a time, it was all I knew.

In 1976, the Honorable Frank J. Battisti ruled that Cleveland
schools were racially segregated. When the Cleveland Public School District implemented desegregation three years later, I was in middle school.
Desegregation meant that black kids would be bused across town to
white schools, white kids would be bused to the black schools, and the
Puerto Rican kids from the near Westside went in both directions. Busing meant that, for the first time, there was going to be more than one
black kid in my school.

I don't remember the angry demonstrations and protests that
reportedly took place, as my family weren't really march-in-the-streets
people. As friends reported how their parents were putting them in parochial or private schools, my mother stuck to her "we are all God's

children under the skin" party line. She was a woman of deep faith and little money. While all five of my siblings attended Catholic school, I had somehow persuaded my parents to allow me to attend public. When busing went into effect, my parents offered me Catholic high school and again I refused.

The first phase of busing reassigned some students for 9th grade, their last year of middle school. I wasn't one of them, which meant I'd be bused for all of high school. In September 1979, I entered 9th grade at Wilbur Wright Junior High School with only half the white kids who attended with me the year before. Very little voluntary mixing with new students took place; in true teen fashion, everyone stuck with their crowd. There were quite a few after-school fights and a lot of assemblies about getting along with each other. I made one black friend that year. She seemed to slide into our group seamlessly.

In the summer of 1980, I found out I would be attending John Hay High School in a part of town I had only visited once before, on a school field trip to the Cleveland Museum of Art Armor Court. That summer, the majority of the kids I'd attended school with for my entire life were being transferred to Griswold Academy, which everyone referred to as "Freedom Academy." Apparently they weren't opposed to attending an unaccredited school and taking a G.E.D. to graduate, as long as they could attend an all-white school.

I probably should have been more worried when school started, but I worked very hard to be blasé and super-cool about the whole thing. I felt sophisticated and tough. Ready for anything. I'm sure there was a fat manila envelope delivered in the weeks leading up to first day of school full of instructions and supply lists and emergency medical forms, but all I remember is receiving the train tickets.

Attending John Hay meant taking the Rapid Transit train to school instead of a school bus. I had only taken the Rapid a handful of times to go downtown to Higbee's with my older sister to shop and get a Frosty. Now getting to school every day would mean a walk to the Rapid, a wait for the Rapid, a ride on the Rapid and then a walk to the school from the University Circle station. This required careful coordination in the morning so no one in our friend group would have to ride alone. Because we were too cool to ride the shuttle from the Rapid to Hay, a daily highlight was crossing the four lanes of rush-hour traffic on Carnegie in the morning. While everyone else made a mad dash, my girlfriend and I would stroll, slowly and belligerently, giving drivers attitude as we crossed against the light.

At first glance, compared to West Tech High School, which held close to 4,000 students, John Hay was small and shabby. And it came with a security guard at the door who checked our IDs every morning. The ID-checking lasted for a few weeks at the beginning of each year and then was abandoned with a laxness that would be unheard of in our post-Columbine world. Then again, it was probably easy to remember 20 white kids in a class of 144.

Inside the classroom, I was back in the majority, as the 13 percent white students translated into 87 percent of the class through the magic of honors courses. The sorting started early in my school career. In second grade, I was classified into what was called "Major Works," and promptly started learning French. My friends and I, with the brutality of the young, broke it down to "Smart Kids" and "Dumb Kids." There must have been Major Works in the all-black schools too, but all through high school my honors classes had a majority of white students.

The only class without an honors section was 10th grade Black Literature, one of the most miserable experiences I can remember in 12 years of schooling. Not because of the content, which at that time was new to me, but because the teacher usually taught the "dumb kids" so the class read aloud from the book one paragraph at a time. Being a "smart kid" meant I'd never experienced such a thing, nor did I know that some kids read so poorly they counted ahead on the paragraphs so they could practice before their turn. Being as snotty and dismissive as I could get away with, I arrogantly propped novels inside my book during this class, reading anything to distance myself from the reality. This class may be what folks imagine Cleveland Public Schools are like, but, aside from this, my reality was AP English, honors French and chemistry. I got a fine education, graduated from college, earned a masters degree and am now a contributing member of society like most of the rest of the class of 1983, who became lawyers, teachers, business owners and professional athletes.

The real education happened outside of class.

Growing up in a working-class, gendered household in the 1970s turned me into a feminist before I knew what to call it. The concept of "women's work" and "men's work" was just the tip of the patriarchal iceberg. As a baby feminist, I was highly attuned to sexist behavior and prejudice against women. What I had never paid any attention to was what it was like to be a minority. I had never noticed that my father called black kids "pickaninnies" or that my brother called Puerto Ricans "spics." I didn't see other kinds of oppression and discrimination. I didn't know what I didn't know.

The first week of school I had trouble with a couple of black girls giving me a hard time, making comments under their breath and sucking their teeth at me. I don't remember what started it or brought it to a head, but back then I wasn't capable of backing down from a confrontation. Bumping turned into shoving, which turned into books slammed to the floor and then stepping up. Thankfully, the assistant principal magically appeared in that way that they do, shut it down, and pulled me into his office. He listened to my outrage at the unjust and unprovoked attack, and kindly explained to me what had happened. The hard stare and tough attitude that I thought said "Don't challenge me" was interpreted here as "I challenge you."

As ignorant as it sounds to be 16 and not recognize that, this was the first time I glimpsed another culture. At sports events, I became one of two white girls on the black side of the bleachers and suddenly could see the unease, wariness and race-consciousness of the all-white teams.

The shifts in my perspective were slow but steady, and shaped who I am today. Walking around in my white skin, even female white skin, gave me the privilege not to see, not to hear, if I didn't want to. Now that I knew some black people, I could hear comments like "Wipe that pop can; you don't know if a black person touched it" for what they were—casual, deeply ingrained prejudice. I started to feel ashamed and embarrassed that my family and neighbors had these racist beliefs. And of myself, that I had never questioned them.

An undisputed benefit of court-ordered busing, among other things, was being given the opportunity to experience what it is like to be in the minority. Just a taste. I would never claim, because of this or any other experience, to know what it's like to be a minority in Cleveland or anywhere else. I will never live in brown skin and cannot know. What I was given, and what I am grateful for, was the chance to understand how narrow and limited my worldview was before I spent three years crossing the mighty Cuyahoga to attend school.

If I hadn't been bused, would it have bothered me when my brother sat with a shotgun on his front porch to "keep the black kids off the grass"? An equal-opportunity hater, he hated Jews, spics, niggers, towel heads and gooks and never missed an opportunity to share his opinions. Busing meant groups of black kids got off the Rapid every day and had to walk past his house to get to West Tech. Seeing as he worked third shift at the factory, 8 a.m. would find him drinking beer on his front porch with his shotgun across his knees to stare down the black kids.

I never witnessed him with his gun, but I remember when he told me how he was "dealing with busing." He was so gleeful that the kids looked scared. I left his house that day feeling sick. I don't think I really believed that racism was "that big of a deal" before that day. It had seemed abstract, harmless, and deep in the past.

Not everyone had a good experience, even the other kids in our class. In fact, 17 of the 20 white kids held their own after-prom over on the West Side. The rest of us danced at Vel's to Atomic Dog.

Many people still blame busing for "ruining" the Cleveland Schools, but for me the experience of getting out of my neighborhood was life altering and incredibly positive. I consider myself lucky. Being bused is the reason I live in a racially and socioeconomically diverse neighborhood and send my child to public school. It's why I attempt to strive for equity and racial and social justice in any work I do. I am grateful not to be white in America but to know that I am.

IV. Cities

The Many Cities of Cleveland

G. M. Donley

I *live in a few of the cities of Cleveland.* All of them coexist on the same land in the northeast corner of Ohio. One Cleveland is geographic, a dot on the map, the place where the Cuyahoga empties into Lake Erie along the Great Lakes' furthest-south coastline, the site of a permanent human settlement with the name "Cleveland" attached to it for the past couple hundred years. It's like a younger version of the dot of Rome or the dot of Kyoto: a constant geographical site where generations of people have lived, worked, fought, played. But the place we think of as Cleveland, Ohio, isn't just that river and the slopes and the buildings and the factories, but also many superimposed and overlapping "mental Clevelands" occupying the same geographic space but operating according to wildly varying visions of "here."

This idea first struck me in a specific way at an odd time: while I was getting robbed on the street one night a dozen years ago. I was, not too cleverly, walking alone in the dark in a fairly deserted neighborhood when two guys appeared from between buildings, pinned me against a parked car, and threatened to shoot me. I didn't actually see a gun, so I started making a calculation as to whether it was worth giving up the $17 in my wallet just in case. I was on my way to a Mekons show for which I had already paid, and that meant my name would already be on the list: no cash required to get in. I'd have to cancel a credit card and get a new driver's license. But the major immediate consequence would be drinking tap water instead of beer. Hmmm. I guess I have a tendency toward abstraction, and so, while this was happening, a new notion appeared in my head: these guys lived in a completely different world than I did, yet the two worlds were grounded in pretty much the same geographic space. We had probably all lived around here for years if not decades, yet it was only at rare moments like this that our two parallel versions of Cleveland mingled together. It didn't seem like it would be fruitful to ask the two guys what they thought about that concept, though, so when one of them yelled he'd blow my f%#*ing head off, I just handed them my wallet.

They ran away around a corner and down a side street. After a minute, I trotted over there (probably foolishly) and looked around to see if they'd tossed the wallet somewhere obvious, but no. I still had my car keys, and I was already more or less at my intended destination, so I decided I might as well go catch the show (only 50 or so people actually showed up—this struck me as hilarious at the time because I had bought in advance only because I feared it would sell out). I borrowed a phone to call my wife to tell her what had happened and that I was okay. Then the club owner, apologetic and fuming, though nothing was any fault of hers, called the police to report the incident and, after the cops came by and talked to me, she kindly gave me a couple of beers.

It was a pretty good show. I didn't think of the muggers except briefly while Sally Timms sang "I Love a Millionaire": I imagined them back in their own world again, sitting on a dumpy, cat-shredded couch, watching TV and getting more wasted. After the show, I walked back to the car more attentively than I had come the other way. As I stepped off the curb into the street, I saw a little plastic toy figure of a man lying at the edge of the pavement, half-crushed. I remembered noticing it earlier that night, just before the two guys appeared, and thinking it was such a striking image that it was probably intended to be a sign of something, if you believe in that kind of stuff, which I don't.

Driving home, I thought back on the various Clevelands I had lived in that day: our Cleveland Heights neighborhood in the morning (a world of moms and dads worrying about kids' school lunches, walking the dog, and getting to work on time); a day cranking through projects in a noisy office in University Circle; an early-evening meeting of my son's scout troop; the world of the bicycle riders I didn't join for a spin that evening because of the other worlds I had to be in; the world of the two thieves who I'm pretty sure were never boy scouts; and the world of people who drive half an hour alone in the dark to stand around in a club with 50 people they mostly don't know, drinking beer and listening to a semi-obscure British punk-era band now veering toward alt-country.

Whenever we talk about a city, it's never one place. Every place is layers of mental places on top of the dirt and grass and wood and concrete. When you say "I'm from Cleveland," whoever you're talking to will conjure up a scenario—as they would if you said "I'm from New Orleans," or "I'm from Budapest." But five people will conjure five different things. Not only does every city have a different meaning for every individual who hears the name, but communities of people who live in that area develop shared ideas that define this place for them. This is how a particular street corner could for one person be the locus of a burgeoning artistic community, while for another it's a faded neighborhood decades past its working-class prime, while for another it's good a place to go rob somebody, and for another it just begs you to open a gourmet restaurant. Same land, same buildings, same air. Different cities.

These are a few of the mental Clevelands I know: The white ethnic blue-collar city that rose in the mid-1800s and has been steadily depopulating since the 1960s. The black blue-collar city that grew for the first few decades of the 20th century and has also been on the downslope since the '60s. The old-money city with New England roots. The multi-ethnic, multicultural, scientific, and medical city that has steadily expanded over the past century. The academic, artistic, and cultural city. The locavore foodie city. The rock and roll city. The classical music city. The it-has-to-be-gritty-to-be-authentic city. The inner-suburban city of gracious leafy streets, family businesses, and shoulder-rubbing pockets of wealth and poverty. The outer suburbanite city of people lured by discounted taxes, visions of spacious lawns, and schools that score high because most of the students aren't in poverty. The urban-rebound city of 20-somethings fleeing bland and wasteful suburban cul-de-sacs and strip malls and moving back into the city core decades after its abandonment by their grandparents' generation. The city of diminished aspirations clinging to shadows of former glory. The city rediscovering its farms, its rivers, its lake. The balance-sheet city with its attractive ratio of affordability to quality of life.

What defines each of these cities is not just geography, but commonalities in what its residents care about. Some of these cities care about race; some don't. For some, income matters; for others, barely at all. One city could be about a neighborhood, another about the lake, another about sexual orientation. Some are about the past, some about the future. Some are about fears, some about dreams. What makes this such a rich, maddening, interesting place is that they're all coexisting among each other, some declining, some ascending, some defending, some innovating, some fleeing, some investing.

In a perverse way, it's good news for the people who want to stick around that the declining Clevelands are declining. Yes, Cleveland occasionally shows up on the list of the poorest cities in America (as defined by the portion of people within its city limits who are in poverty), but at the same time, the raw number of impoverished people has been going down for decades. It's just that the total population within the city limits has sometimes fallen even faster, so the city remains poor by statistical proportion. Instead of 200,000 poor people out of 800,000 total, it's 120,000 out of 400,000 total, plus coyotes.

That is largely because the blue-collar city no longer offers the same opportunities it once did, and the social groups that once flocked to blue-collar Cleveland can no longer find so many blue-collar jobs. (Yes, there has also been white and black and Hispanic and Asian migration of urban-core dwellers to further-out places, but if the low-skilled jobs were still here, an influx of new residents would have continued to fill in the inner city.)

If you can't build one of those increasingly rare blue-collar careers, there are three options if you're a blue-collar city resident: retrain for the jobs that are here (thus staying in place but leaving blue-collar Cleveland for one of the other Clevelands), physically leave blue-collar Cleveland for blue-collar jobs elsewhere, or be unemployed in Cleveland. Option 2 causes the population of Cleveland to go down, leaving a higher proportion of lower-income folks, but in ever-dwindling numbers. It would not take much of an influx of new middle-class residents to quickly tip the numerical balance decisively back toward growth, simply because there are so few people left within the city limits.

The sense of panic and despair about perceived decline may arise because Cleveland is actually a young city. We're still in our first big cycle of building and obsolescence—since it hasn't gone around more than once yet, it doesn't look like a cycle to us, but like the downslope of a one-time rise-and-fall. But everything you build is going to either wear out or need substantial restoration every couple of generations—the question is just what to do when it gets to that point. So put it in perspective. Rome in the time of Michelangelo was just rebounding from a century during which much of the city had reverted to a wilder state. Packs of wolves roamed the hills. Every building in that city is built on the remains of something older, which itself is built on something older still. There are topographic and logical reasons for Rome to be where it is. Same with Cleveland. But future Clevelands, just like the succession of Romes built on that same land, will reflect the lives of the people of their own times. There will be reminders of the past, buildings, and even, sometimes, entire old neighborhoods that survive—but new mental Clevelands will be layered over those physical environments.

Patterns will change. Though Cleveland originally grew from concentrations of ethnically homogenous immigrants, new Clevelands will emerge through the shared values of its residents: there are people of all backgrounds who want an interesting, walkable neighborhood with diverse options for everything from housing to food. They'll settle in a community here because they can get that at a modest price. Ask a random resident of Cleveland Heights or Lakewood why they choose to live there: typically it's a combination of the affordability of beautiful housing, the scale and character of the streets, the quirky local businesses, arts and culture, and the fact that their neighbor probably does not look just like them. A sense of common identity binds them together, but this time it's not racial or ethnic identity.

It's interesting to compare the original settlement pattern of this landscape with what might likely happen with a repopulation. The first villages grew up along the river mouth and on the nearby bluffs. As industry evolved in the pre-auto era, dense pockets of worker housing clustered naturally around the factories, also close to the river. When the rail and trolley systems allowed, neighborhoods grew up along those corridors. Then the post-World War II highway system drew people much further out—and eventually urban density was much diluted as businesses followed the residents and more residents followed businesses. On the global scale, transportation advances and remote industrialization steadily siphoned off to other parts of the world work that had once been done in American central cities, and thus, as people left the city for the suburbs or the Sun Belt, no one else moved in to fill their former neighborhoods.

Repopulation will not cluster around riverside factories this time, and not right along the heaviest rail and highway corridors either because today's predominant transportation modes allow people to get a little distance away from that noise and grit. What will likely happen instead is new residents will fill in the most topographically desirable parts of the city nearest the lake first: north of Chester between downtown and University Circle, Edgewater and Ohio City; then the slopes of the Fairfax neighborhood with its easy access to University Circle and Shaker Square. Revitalization would build outward block-by-block from the strongest core neighborhoods and commercial districts until, eventually, expanding pockets ran into each other to reconstitute continuous urban vitality.

Of course this sounds familiar: it's how cities are always formed. The old town of Ohio City was eventually wrapped into rival town Cleveland. Once-remote Idlewood Village is now part of Cleveland Heights. But this time, instead of spreading out and linking up over pristine fields and woods, we're recycling and repurposing land developed generations ago. Archaeologists looking back at this in a thousand years will see it as a new layer, a time when the community reimagined how the land would be used.

The standard scenario of gentrification has new residents coming into a long-neglected low-income area, and as they buy and fix up properties, the rents begin to go up, thus forcing out the former residents. In the 1990s, Boston's South End gentrified, but the statistical decline in the number of low-income residents wasn't necessarily always people being forced out. As the neighborhood became home to more people with more income, opportunities arose for some locals to earn more income and rise out of poverty. Those people were able to change worlds from impoverished Boston to rejuvenating Boston without actually leaving the neighborhood. Statistically, it looked like low-income people had been displaced by people with more money, but some of them were the same people, just making more income.

Given the right opportunities, how could people in the low-income city stay where they are and become residents of a different Cleveland with a more positive trajectory? First, we should note that there are a couple of important differences between Boston's South End and Cleveland: one, the buildings of Boston's South End were mostly durable brick apartments and townhouses, where in Cleveland we have mostly freestanding wood-frame homes that are less likely to have survived decades of deferred maintenance; and two, even before the decades of population decline, Cleveland was never as dense as Boston (and that was part of the reason New Englanders moved here). In earlier times, as cities cycled through decline and renewal, the amount of land affected was relatively small because the places were very dense. Now we're seeing our first streetcar communities and automobile-scaled places start to wear out.

What that means is that, after neighborhoods have been neglected for a couple of generations, we are left with scattered wood-frame houses among a lot of vacant lots, and those lots are fairly large. Opportunity for rebirth can be found in the best remaining buildings, but perhaps even more so in the spaces between. Lots of space, not that many people. The opportunities range from using vacant land for agriculture until such time as some other use becomes viable, to creating new corridors of greenway around which future redevelopment would be built, to starting with a clean slate and building new commercial uses or neighborhood architectural forms that reflect the priorities of current times.

These land-reclamation scenarios offer possibilities not just for people bringing investment from outside the neighborhoods but also for inner-city residents. Collaborative neighborhood farming projects, for example, may not provide much income at first, but they substantially improve quality of life and provide skills and understanding that people can continue to use to improve their lives for as long as they live. This is happening already, for example through the city's various urban gardening projects. Many of these first steps take place outside the formal dollar economy: knowing how to produce food and cook good meals are two skills that add enormous value to life independent of the exchange of money. There are often ways to achieve worthy ends that don't require a lot of dollars but instead directly improve lives through skills and knowledge. With Cleveland's available open land, our still-viable utility and transportation infrastructure, some targeted investments, and strong motivation on the part of residents, the seeds of regrowth are here.

There's certainly a role for the government in this beyond just the mandated basic services: thoughtful efforts toward building public amenities can establish an enhanced quality of life that not only is an end in itself but can serve as a catalyst for more investment. The library systems and Metroparks come to mind. And the relatively small amount

113

of money provided by the Cuyahoga Arts and Culture cigarette tax has paid off exponentially in both large institutional strength and neighborhood-level arts activity that has made life in Cuyahoga County noticeably more vibrant.

But, fundamentally, rebuilding our city isn't a grand-scale project. It's a you-and-me project. That's how it works. Before anything happens, somebody has to care enough to make an effort even knowing it might not pay off. Just take a look around: the Conways decided to open a brewpub on moribund Market Square 25 years ago and now West 25th Street is bustling. Cindy Barber and Mark Leddy opened the Beachland Ballroom in 2000 and sparked the reinvention of the entire Waterloo Road commercial district. University Circle is not only home to museum expansions and hospital construction, but it's adding new housing and creating a completely new urban space around the intersection of Mayfield Road and Euclid Avenue. Look out the window of the Shaker Rapid at 79th street and you'll see greenhouses and a manicured path in the woods where there used to be piles of garbage. Mansfield Frazier's little vineyard on Hough Avenue shows how a neighborhood notorious for riots in the 1960s can reinvent itself, and that may be part of why, a few blocks away, the city is restoring historic League Park (where Cy Young pitched for Cleveland 120 years ago). After decades of stubborn pioneering by individuals in Tremont, that area has evolved into a lively place to wander leisurely on a summer evening (or dash from restaurant to gallery to bar in the winter). A couple of neighbors put some effort into their properties, start raising the expectation a little bit, and if it catches on pretty soon the whole block is taking more pride and looking better. People want to be on that street. Or maybe the next street over, which costs a little less but isn't quite as nice yet—but with a little work . . . that's how a good neighborhood grows.

You can almost hear some people muttering, "Nobody wants to live in the city. You're taking your life in your hands to go to those places. Downtown is dying. You're wasting your time. Throwing good money after bad." Blah, blah, blah. If you're in the city or the older suburbs and working to make your place better, the persistent drone of that kind of talk can be dispiriting—but keep in mind that the people who talk like that aren't making the new cities of Cleveland. You are.

So what about my two thieves? How would they fit into a new Cleveland? The question I asked myself back then is what I ask myself now: How did they get to that mental place? Here are two young guys who could be contributing to the community in some way, but instead they are wasting whatever potential they might have, and wasting some of the city's potential at the same time. It's infuriating. So why? Maybe it had to do with the possibilities they could see for themselves. During Cleveland's boom-town years, say, from the 1880s through the 1920s, people moved here for opportunity, and even the poorest families coming to work the most menial jobs had aspirations of moving up so their kids would move up. It could happen, and did, over and over.

Jump ahead a few generations. Those ladders that promised the chance to climb up from poverty now seem to be missing the bottom few rungs. Base-level jobs that lead to better jobs just aren't here in great numbers. On top of that, over the past 50 years, many city residents who made it into the middle class or above have left the inner city for suburbs or other regions, so there aren't a lot of role models for the people left in the neighborhood. There may not be a clear path for how to make something of yourself in mainstream society. Mix in a certain lack of imagination and for some, the best opportunity may seem to be selling drugs or robbing people. Maybe that's what's going on. I don't know.

On the upside, these two at least showed some willingness to take a risk, however misguided. If guys like that could have their eyes opened to other pathways for their aggressive energies, maybe they would think of something better to do on a Monday night than go out robbing people. Maybe not. But one thing's for sure: their Cleveland is a dying city, and just about any of the other cities of Cleveland would offer a chance at a brighter future. So here's hoping they take a look around at their possibilities and conclude that it's time to move to a better place.

Remaking Buffalo's Waterfront: Lessons for the Rest of the Rust Belt

Edward McClelland

I *n the summer of 2005,* I took a boat trip up the Buffalo River. I had a hard time just finding the river, which was hidden beneath elevated highways and closed off from the city by fences and factories.

Once I made my way to the docks and boarded a motor boat, I spent the next hour on a body of water that appeared moribund in every sense: aquatically, recreationally, and industrially. The river caught fire in 1968 and was labeled biologically dead by the Environmental Protection Agency. Not much life had returned since. Empty grain elevators, bearing the names of defunct local breweries, towered over both banks, as tall and as grim as housing projects, remnants of the years before the St. Lawrence Seaway opened in 1959, when Buffalo was the transfer point for agricultural products between the Great Lakes and the Atlantic Ocean. Now, no one had any use for the silos, and they were too expensive to tear down.

Even Buffalo's better-known bodies of water, Lake Erie and the Niagara River, were isolated from a city which owed its existence to their presence. The lakefront was dominated by the brownfield remains of Bethlehem Steel, which closed in 1983, and by the Outer Harbor, a port little used since the Seaway allowed ships to bypass Buffalo. In the 1950s, infamous urban planner Robert Moses ran the New York State Thruway right along the Niagara River. At the time, Buffalonians didn't mind. The lake and the river were seen as alimentary canals for the steel mills and tanneries. Nobody wanted to live alongside such filth.

"For several generations, the population didn't think of the waterways as community assets, because [people] weren't connected to the waterfront," said Jill Jedlicka, executive director of Buffalo Niagara Riverkeeper, an organization that advocates for cleaning up Western New York's waters. "Twenty-five years ago, I don't think you could access the Buffalo River legally."

Buffalo is the mother of Great Lakes cities—the first to rise to prominence, the first to establish the template of ethnic neighborhoods anchored by churches and taverns, the first to decline from industrial glory. And now it is demonstrating how a Rust Belt city can transform its waterways from polluted industrial resources to fishable, swimmable, kayakable lifestyle amenities. Nearly a decade after I took that spooky boat trip, the Buffalo River is the site of concerts, hockey tournaments, parks, and brand new restaurants.

The renaissance of Buffalo's waterways began at the mouth of the Buffalo River, which the state-run Erie County Harbor Development Corporation has been attempting to transform into a Great Lakes version of Baltimore's Inner Harbor, even calling it by the same name. This was the birthplace of modern Buffalo—where the Erie Canal ended its 363-mile run from the Hudson River to Lake Erie.

In 2004, U.S. Rep. Brian Higgins obtained $350 million to rebuild the Inner Harbor from the New York Power Authority. The NYPA had made millions from power generated by Niagara Falls, so Higgins negotiated a relicensing agreement that returned the money to his hometown. The Inner Harbor project began with Canalside, where construction crews excavated 320 feet of the Erie Canal terminus and transformed it into a boat slip. Three World War II ships are anchored at a naval park, and a livery rents kayaks for river excursions. On Central Wharf, a wooden boardwalk, seagulls dive for French fries from an open-air restaurant. Coming soon are a children's museum, a three-story restaurant, and an outdoor skating rink three times the size of Rockefeller Center's: Buffalo will not be outdone in winter amusements.

Typical for Buffalo, there's not a lot of space to work with: the looming Skyway slices through the sunlight and separates Canalside from downtown. But the progress has been spreading up the river and down the lakefront. This spring will see the opening of One Canalside, an office building and hotel in an old state office building. Across the street, Buffalo Sabres owner Terry Pegula is building Harbor Center, with two indoor ice rinks, a hotel, and an eight-story underground parking garage.

The Harbor Development Corporation recently gained control of the 400-acre Outer Harbor, which will become a state park, with the city's only Lake Erie bathing beach. (The other half will be taken over by Gracious Living, a Canadian company that produces molded Adirondack chairs.)

"It is the last stretch of land that we have not been able to connect to the rest of the community," said Robert Gioia, chairman of the Corporation. "There have been several starts and stops, but there really wasn't the momentum we've seen over the last five years, starting with Canalside."

Canalside was also the key to opening the Buffalo River to development. A $44 million cleanup, paid for by the Environmental Protection Agency and private industry, is dredging the river of sediment deposited by decades of producing steel, coke, pesticides, and dyes.

The cleanup was the result of 25 years of pressure from Buffalo Niagara Riverkeeper, an environmental organization that believes water is more valuable to a modern city when it's clean than when it's dirty. The Riverkeeper calls that transformation the Blue Economy Initiative, using the slogan "From Rust to Blue: Buffalo Niagara's NEW Economy."

"For Western New York and for Buffalo, we've been saying that water defined our history, and water's going to define our future," Jedlicka said. "For the longest time, our natural assets have been seen as liabilities because they were polluted. The health of the water really affects the health of your economy. We're a community in transition. We want to transform away from the tradition of the Rust Belt, so the cost of a local economy is not to destroy your natural resource. We've been working on restoration for ten years. This does not always have to be a toxic river. This is a working waterway."

Doug Swift, a local entrepreneur, decided that clean water and a connection to Canalside made the Buffalo River an attractive place to open an entertainment complex called Riverworks. This winter, Swift held a 120-team outdoor hockey tournament along the river. By Memorial Day, he plans to open a restaurant in the six-cylinder Grange

League Federation silo, which has not stored grain since the early 1960s. (Further upriver is Silo City, a climbing wall/art installation. As Swift notes, Buffalo was the birthplace of the grain silo, and has the nation's largest collection: "we want to use silos as a combination of public art and billboard.")

The Corporation is also spending $5 million to project light shows on the grain elevators. Modeled on the lighting of the Eiffel Tower and the Bay Bridge, and hearkening back to Buffalo's past as "The City of Light" at the electrified 1901 Pan-American Exposition, the shows have attracted fascinated crowds and national attention.

"They've been talking about waterfront development here since the 1950s," Swift said. "Really, in the past four or five years, Buffalo's effort to reinvent itself is taking hold. Canalside has triggered major investment. We consider ourselves an extension of that, and want to start making linkages."

John Norquist, the former Milwaukee mayor and current president and CEO of the Council for New Urbanism (which is holding its annual conference in Buffalo this year) once said that Robert Moses's "dead gray hands are still strangling the city of Buffalo." As a result of the Thruway, Buffalo's Riverside Park—the last urban space designed by Frederick Law Olmsted, with a white block casino, a classical bathhouse for the swimming pool and stone steps terracing the grassy slope to the waterfront—was cut off from its namesake. Now, to walk from Riverside Park to the river, pedestrians have to cross a skyway over six lanes of traffic just to reach a twenty-foot strip of grass between the Thruway and the river. In modern Buffalo, this is a riverfront park. The idea of rerouting the Thruway off the riverfront began with a neighborhood organization called Rediscover Riverside. At first, it seemed as crazy as cleaning up the Buffalo River or building a restaurant in a grain silo must have sounded. But now, it's being talked about as part of a long-term plan for reclaiming the waterfront. The Robert Moses Parkway, which hugs the waterfront south of Niagara Falls, is already scheduled for demolition. Someday, that could happen in Buffalo, too.

"It would be great," said the Riverkeeper's Jedlicka, "as a 50-year vision, to get that off the waterfront."

Asked what Buffalo should do with its water-blocking highways, Norquist said, "I'd tear 'em all down, as fast as you can. The Skyway carries 40,000 cars a day. You don't need that. The Thruway could become a multi-lane boulevard. You don't need to have a high-speed highway separating a beautiful city from the water, and they'd instantly have the best lakefront on Lake Erie."

Norquist made his political career as an opponent of freeways. As mayor, he blocked the extension of the Park East Freeway to Lake Michigan, and built a Riverwalk that resulted in a downtown housing boom, including 28-story and 30-story apartment buildings.

Tearing down and rerouting highways would likely be a multi-billion dollar task. Robert Gioia refers to the Skyway and the Thruway as "lessons learned," but realizes they are on the waterfront to stay, at least for the near future. For now, Buffalo has to do a better job of establishing "cross-connectivities" between the city and the lake, he said.

But what would opening up the waterfront mean to the people who live down there now? Would they be forced to leave if the land becomes more desirable? When Bonnie Eschborn founded Rediscover Riverside, she was rooting for gentrification. Eschborn grew up in Riverside before the Thruway was laid down, when the neighborhood was home to blue-collar Poles and Italians, many employed at the nearby GM engine plant in Tonawanda. The highway provided them a route to the suburbs, and they were replaced by lower-class whites. Most residents are renters, the average household income is $24,356 a year, and the average owner-occupied house is worth $59,300. The crime rate is nearly triple the statewide average. This less than a hundred yards from one of North America's most storied rivers. But the salient feature of Riverside is no longer water, it's a loud, dirty, six-lane road, which has turned out to be even less appealing than the polluted riverfront it replaced.

"Who wants to sit here and listen to this?" Eschborn said. "This is not peaceful."

Now that the river is not so polluted, Eschborn estimated that rerouting the Thruway would double property values in Riverside to the same level as those in Tonawanda, where the road swings away from the river and onto Grand Island.

"People just want to be by the water," Eschborn said. "If you see all these people wanting to be by the waterfront, you'd think [Mayor] Byron [Brown] would be on top of it."

The largest parcel of lakefront property in the Buffalo area is the 1,600-acre Bethlehem Steel site in Lackawanna, directly south of the city, where Lake Erie begins to narrow into the Niagara River. The mill closed in 1983, and the grounds have been reverting to nature ever since, with whitetail deer bounding through meadows of chicory, goldenrod, yarrow, and peppergrass. As a brownfield, still littered with slag pots, the site is too polluted for housing or recreation. Until recently, the only enterprise operating on the site was up in the air: Steel Winds, 14 wind turbines gathering breezes from Lake Erie. The turbines generate 50 million kilowatt hours of electricity each year, enough to power 9,000 homes, and have become symbols of Buffalo, appearing in establishing shots during Bills games.

"We have the wind," said Assistant Operations Manager Stephen Slack. "This is one of the first urban wind farms. Would you rather put a house on a brownfield, or would you rather build something you have to go 80 meters into the air to work on?"

Nonetheless, Bethlehem Steel is off-limits to the public, surrounded by a fence hung with "No Trespassing" signs. And its beach looks like a landscape from the post-apocalyptic movie *The Road* (which was filmed on Lake Erie.) Metal glitters in the ragged cliff, and the sand looks gray. You might want to swim here, but you wouldn't want to get out of the water.

"Where's the green? Where's the moss? Where's the algae?" Slack asked. "You can see the cliff face. It just doesn't look natural to me. There's lines in it that sparkle. So what is it?"

In the summer of 2013, the Canadian manufacturer Welded Tube opened a 40-acre factory to build steel pipe. To accommodate the new enterprise, and to make it easier for other businesses to locate there, the state of New York spent $4.4 million to reroute a rail line through the site. Local officials hope Welded Tube is the beginning of the lakefront's return to an industrial role it played for most of the 20th Century.

"I heard lot of people say, 'Why are you wasting any time and effort on the old Bethlehem Steel site? No one is ever going to move there,'" Erie County Executive Mark C. Poloncarz told the *Buffalo News*. "Well, now we have a $40 million industry on forty acres."

Buffalo is doing more than any Great Lakes city to reconnect with its waterfront after generations of neglect, alienation, and industrial abuse. But it's only the most aggressive example of a regional effort that's also taking place in Milwaukee, Cleveland, Detroit, Chicago, and Toronto. Redeveloping Great Lakes waterfronts was the subject of a March 13 symposium at the Chicago Architecture Foundation, "Designing for Life along the Water's Edge."

In Chicago, Mayor Rahm Emanuel is trying to reintegrate the Chicago River back into the life of the city by extending the Riverwalk along its entire main branch. Emanuel's plan calls for six stations, each devoted to a different method of interacting with the water—kayaking, dining, a floating garden, an ecology learning center, a boat launch. Emanuel's administration also built a canoe and kayak livery on each branch of the river.

Along the lakefront, the city has extended Lake Shore Drive through U.S. Steel South Works, which closed in 1992, in preparation for a development which is expected to have 13,575 new homes, 17.5 million square feet of retail space—and revive the economic fortunes of South Chicago, a neighborhood that has struggled ever since it lost the mill.

In Detroit, the Riverfront Conservancy built a three-and-a-half mile river walk, with the help of General Motors, which donated land behind the Renaissance Center, and the state, which dedicated a new park to former Michigan governor William Milliken. Long-term plans call for extending the river walk to Belle Isle.

Cleveland just announced it will lease 28 acres of empty lakefront behind the Browns' football stadium to developers who plan to build 1,000 apartments, a school, and retail arcades. On the Cuyahoga River, the Flats East Bank project will bring restaurants, a hotel, and an office building to an unused stretch of riverbank. The Northeast Ohio Regional Sewer District is spending $3 billion to clean up sewage discharge that sullies Lake Erie after heavy rains.

"In Cleveland, there's a tremendous pent-up desire to capitalize on our waterfront and drive our city back to prosperity," *Plain Dealer* architecture critic Steven Litt said at the symposium. "We've walled off miles of lakefront behind highways, railroads, water treatment plants, and private yacht clubs on public land. In all those years, there's not been a smidgen of private development on our waterfront."

That's exactly where Buffalo was in the mid-2000s. The entire Rust Belt can take a lesson from what they've done about it.

Attention Would-Be Urban Homesteaders: Think Before You Buy

Gordon Young

T*he national media,* no doubt conditioned by the exorbitant cost of living on the two coasts, loves tales of houses in flyover country selling for the price of a crappy used car and the plucky urban homesteaders who buy them. So does the public. A recent BuzzFeed story by Drew Philip about his Herculean efforts to restore a $500 house in Detroit attracted more than 1.4 million views. "The city is filled with these structures, houses whose yellowy eyes seem to follow you," Philip wrote. "It would be only one house out of thousands, but I wanted to prove it could be done, prove that this American vision of torment could be built back into a home."

Commendable? You bet. Inspiring? Absolutely. But Philip's reclamation project should also serve as a warning for anyone who has ever fantasized about snapping up a house on eBay for three figures in a Rust Belt city like Cleveland, Youngstown, or Saginaw. It's easy to envision yourself in a pair of Carhartts and a flannel shirt sanding hardwood floors, modernizing the kitchen, and planting apple trees in the front yard. But as Philip illustrates, you should also be prepared for the less savory tasks, like spending frigid winters without heat, removing every imaginable form of debris (including "literal piles of human shit"), buying a shotgun, and being prepared to use it.

If you're not financially stable, committed to years of hard work, and willing to deal with the frustrations that come with life in a city that used to build things, your psyche and your bank account will take a big hit. And you might end up hurting the very place you were trying to help when you call it quits and walk away.

I found this out for myself when I returned to my hometown of Flint, Michigan, to buy a house in the summer of 2009 after living in San Francisco for more than a decade. The chance to rediscover a simpler life and help spur the revival of America's industrial heartland pulled me like a magnet back to the Vehicle City. I longed to escape a toxic mortgage and do my part to help the town where four generations of my family lived, and I enjoyed a happy childhood in the seventies and eighties, despite Flint's socioeconomic swan dive. But my three-year quest, fueled by good intentions, nostalgia, and delusional thinking, didn't go quite as planned.

I quickly discovered that you get what you pay for, even in Flint. The city is infamous for crime and blight. It's labeled the most dangerous city in America, based on FBI statistics, and approximately one-third is abandoned. Michael Moore's unexpectedly popular documentary *Roger & Me* chronicled the devastating impact of General Motors layoffs on the city. But that doesn't mean there are no vibrant, well-maintained neighborhoods. Areas like Mott Park and Woodcroft Estates have great houses ranging from the quaint to the palatial. A friend in Flint recently bought a Cape Cod in the sylvan College Cultural area. It's a handsome, 75-year-old wood-shingled specimen with five bedrooms, three full baths, and a paneled library where Sherlock Holmes would feel comfortable. Birch trees dot the backyard. The price? Just $70,000, a steal by big-city standards, but hardly the stuff of pocket-change dreams.

In more humble neighborhoods, homes have inevitably been feasted upon by scrappers in search of any metal they can sell. Strips of aluminum siding have been peeled off, copper plumbing and wiring ripped out, water heaters and fixtures absconded with. Even doorknobs aren't safe. Materials and labor for home improvement projects are market rate, so the cost of restoring a run-down American Foursquare in a struggling area is comparable to fixing one up in a more prosperous location. If you don't have serious do-it-yourself skills, you could go broke fast. A few replacement windows could easily top the purchase price of a house.

Oh, don't forget that trying to fix up the house while living somewhere else is a bad idea. An unguarded house in the process of restoration is the dream of enterprising scrappers. Once you start major repairs, you better be camping inside or living nearby. A part-time vanity project this ain't.

Then there are the hidden costs and drawbacks of owning a fix-er-upper in a depopulating city with double-digit unemployment. Taxes and fees are higher to offset declining local revenues. Detroit, for example, has the highest property taxes in the country. And Flint's emergency manager—granted control of the city by the governor to deal with a burgeoning budget deficit—recently hiked water, sewer, and garbage collection rates, and imposed a new fee to pay for streetlights. Home and auto insurance policies also tend to be more expensive. The same goes for utilities.

The prospect of these low-cost houses appreciating in value anytime soon is hardly a sure thing. These are often older residences with small rooms and a single bath. Local schools are underfunded and underperforming. Municipal and state budget cuts result in reduced city services like police and fire protection. Sure, you could get lucky and land in a neighborhood that stages a turnaround, but if you expect to resell at a profit after lovingly restoring your home, a trip to Vegas may be a better bet. I hear blackjack has the best odds.

Thankfully, cities recognize that the purchase price is just the first step in transforming an abandoned house into a real home. In the Rust Belt and beyond, there are local initiatives offering property for less than the cost of a gym membership. Gary, Indiana, with its 10,000 abandoned homes, has a lottery to sell houses for $1 to residents who meet certain financial and residency requirements in an effort to reinvigorate a city crushed by deindustrialization. "My target would be to sell 50 houses a year," Mayor Karen Freeman-Wilson told *The New York Times.* "We're getting these people to contribute as taxpayers. They can be part of the group that moves out, or they can be part of the group that invests."

But the program wisely demands a minimum income of $35,250 for individuals, at least $1,000 in savings, and the demonstrated ability to rehabilitate the house. Gary's mayor estimates that each home in the lottery needs $20,000 to $50,000 in renovations. In other words, that first dollar is just the start of an extended financial commitment.

It took me a few years of fruitless house hunting, back-of-the-envelope financial calculations, and some real soul searching to realize that I had no business purchasing a house in Flint. The last thing the city needed was another financially challenged homeowner, even one whose heart was in the right place. This wasn't some lark. The residents I met in Flint restoring old homes were hardcore. They were in it for the long haul and willing to part with tens of thousands of dollars to stake their claim to this troubled spot on the Michigan map. I also met well-meaning folks who couldn't hack it. They gave up on their renovation dreams, leaving empty houses behind. This was clearly not the stuff of fantasy.

While it lacks the emotional appeal of stories about the young idealists who venture back to these struggling cities, land banks are a more far-reaching and clear-eyed attempt to help places like Flint. They don't focus on getting residents into abandoned housing; instead, they concentrate on eliminating empty structures.

Admittedly, the land-bank approach appeals more to the head than the heart. It requires cities to let go of the past and admit they might never regain the growing populations, thriving economies, and broad middle-class prosperity of the post-war boom. Though it's not an economic plan that will generate new jobs, it is a logical step toward stabilization and it lays the groundwork for the future. It wasn't very satisfying, but at one point I thought that paying to tear down a land-bank house in Flint would be the best way to give back to my hometown. There was one problem; I couldn't afford it. Demolition costs $9,000 a pop.

In the end, I was fortunate enough to help Flint in my own small way. I befriended a man named Sherman McCathern, the energetic pastor of Joy Tabernacle Church, located in my old neighborhood of Civic Park. He battles crime, house flippers, and the forces of economic decline while ministering to a flock beset by unemployment and heartache. Not long after I reluctantly gave up my quest for home ownership, he told me that someone had donated a house to the church. The pastor, in turn, had given it to a church member nicknamed P-Nut, a young guy with a family who was trying to rebuild his life after a stint in jail. But the house needed work and there was no way to pay for it. The solution seemed obvious. I donated the money I had saved for a Flint house to help with the renovations.

There's no silver bullet that will solve the problem of abandoned houses in America's shrinking cities. Well-meaning Rust Belt expatriates like me can lend a hand. Dedicated urban homesteaders can save some houses with money, carpentry skills, and sheer force of will. Innovative projects like Detroit's Write A House, which gives a renovated home to writers who move to the Motor City, can play a role in stabilizing neighborhoods. But the staggering number of empty houses means that these laudable efforts are only a small part of the solution. Land banks and other initiatives to demolish the structures that no one wants will have a far greater impact. It's something that people on the front lines like Pastor McCathern understand, even as they fight to save their neighborhoods.

"I accept that we're going to have to tear down some of these houses," he told me on a hot summer day as we stood in the parking lot of his church. "It's like we have to purge Civic Park before we can bring it back."

This Ain't City Chicken: The Geography of Authenticity

Ben Schulman

*I*n *his 1996 essay,* "A Little Taste of Something More Exotic: The Imaginative Geographies of Everyday Life," geographer Jon May wrote about the embrace of ethnic foods by the "cultural class"—what Richard Florida would later popularize as The Creative Class—as a process of the "consumption of the exotic." Riffing on Edward Said's concept of imaginative geographies, May recognized how eating exotic foods offers admission—or the appearance of admission—into a foreign and, perhaps, more exciting world.

This consumption is enhanced by geography. While it's one thing to eat Indian food by purchasing many of the readily available ingredients or pre-made meals from a standard supermarket, the act of eating Indian food becomes *real* when doing so alongside people of Indian descent in Indian neighborhoods. "The authentically exotic is that which is bought in places where only the 'original' consumers of these foods come to eat or shop, lending the food itself an added degree of 'authenticity,'" May wrote.

Goldfinch American, the controversial new restaurant on Detroit's Southwest side, spins off May's conception of authenticity. At Goldfinch, it's not so much the fare being served that tenders a portal to the authentic (according to their website, they offer the bespoke-yet-vague-enough-to-eat-anywhere "experimental micro restaurant concept serving progressive modern american [sic] food"), but the literal landscape in which the restaurant resides.

Goldfinch American is selling the chance to consume an *authentic* landscape—an "ostensibly unattractive street trash-lined and zipping with cars," surrounded by "laundromats, taquerias, a beautiful park, abandoned fortresses and neighborhoods thick with life lived fully."

Authenticity may be a nebulous concept, but its signifiers are readily identifiable; like obscenity, you know it when you see it. Whether filtered through the lens of Jane Jacobs, ethnic enclaves, the reimagining of industrial places, or even in the pastiche of new urbanist developments, authenticity emerges as a cultural reconstruction of "traditional" space.

As cities are defined less and less by the productive capacity of hard labor, and more so by the consumptive possibilities imbibed in by its post-industrial labor pool, authenticity becomes an aesthetic. In her book *Naked City: The Death and Life of Authentic Urban Places*, the writer Sharon Zukin examines how formerly working-class or industrial neighborhoods in New York, such as Williamsburg and Harlem, have become "great places for consuming authenticity" as they are further divorced from the acts of production that once defined their being.

The Rust Belt shines with the allure of the authentic. Its atrophied industrial muscles beg for redevelopment that reflects upon the past as present. The Rust Belt Romantic, as a style, appropriates nostalgia for spaces of physical production via the embrace of industrial chic. Perceived authenticity is cool.

Rust Belt Romanticism creates a city in which the act of consuming "life lived fully" has a very real effect on the ownership of urban space, offered to those "selective buyers with eyes for amenities, authenticity, and aesthetics," as Richard Florida has written.

These are consumptive geographies, wherein authenticity is commoditized and reduced to an amenity. These geographies are the spatial equivalent of a reproduction, echoing Walter Benjamin's "The Work of Art in the Age of Mechanical Reproduction" wherein the cityscape, while flavored by nostalgia for a past never experienced by its purveyors or consumers, is "lacking in one element: its presence in time and space, its unique existence at the place where it happens to be."

Of course, the irony in selling authenticity as an amenity is that each instance of authenticity—and how it applies to a particular place—is weakened through its commodification. Authenticity as a commodity

132

flow washes over cities everywhere as a tool for redevelopment.

While Detroit's Southwest Side, home of Goldfinch American, isn't quite as fragmented by vacancy as other parts of the city, it isn't difficult to find the "authentic" Detroit of derelict parcels and abandoned lots in its midst. It isn't hard, along the streets of Detroit's Mexicantown, to find, as the Goldfinch website states, "fucking pigeons" who descend upon the corner of Clark and Vernor to gorge on that what's left behind by "weary travelers [who] hurriedly board the lumbering buses squealing to a stop by the bus shelter, sending fried chicken and fries flying into the sidewalk."

Goldfinch American craftily—and crudely—markets all this as an amenity, self-aware of the fact it is selling something beyond just its $108/5-course fixed price meal and cocktail pairings.

Some have castigated Goldfinch American for exploiting its very own neighborhood, its very own city. Such complaints ignore the fact that the restaurant simply occupies a space on the continuum of the commodity flow of authenticity. Having left its imprint on the former industrial pockets of New York and other locales, the flow of authenticity pushes forward, snaking through rusty cities and susceptible landscapes everywhere.

Jon May viewed the consumption of food as an opening to experience the "other." But at a place like Goldfinch American, it's not the food that's "othered," it's the city itself. To invoke a more authentic culinary term, this ain't city chicken.

Dispatches from the Rust Belt

The Grapes of Hough

Daniel J. McGraw

Walking up to Mansfield Frazier's house at E. 66th Street and Hough Avenue in Cleveland, one's mind wonders a bit about what you are seeing and why, especially if you are white guy with a suburban upbringing. His house is new and pretty big and very much the type you find in sprawltopia. But I find myself looking across the street at Grandma's Mini-Mart, a convenience store that looks like it has been shut down for a while. A lady hanging out the upstairs windows is shouting to some guys next to parked cars on the street. Not anything too weird, but certainly not something you see on a cul-de-sac in Mentor.

Boarded-up old residential buildings and lots of vacant lots are close by Mansfield's house in all four directions. Just a few blocks west is the urban industrial wasteland of E. 55th Street, where they used to make all sorts of metallic things that helped make bigger metallic things, back when Cleveland had some might and swagger and style going for it. Proof of that is the long-abandoned Richman Brothers factory on 55th, where they made suits for the factory guys to wear to christenings and movies with the sweetheart at the Hippodrome downtown and court dates with the judges.

It's not that it seems unsafe down here, it's just that there doesn't seem to be much of anything functional left. Buildings with plywood on the windows and lots of broken glass around makes the mind lean that way.

But Mansfield's house is fairly new, built in 2000, and there are a few others around like his, which makes this part of Cleveland even more confusing. These new homes began popping up in the mid-1990s, when the economy was decent and the banks were throwing money around more than they do now. The houses do look quite nice, well-appointed three-bedroom homes with no bars on the windows. But I learn later that new constructions have pretty much stopped. Some think the banks have pulled out the red pen again in the Hough neighborhood and others like it in Cleveland.

And if you want even more neighborhood confusion, look to the lot catercorner to Mansfield's house and notice the 14 rows of grapes growing. He is growing grapes on this lot and making wine called "Chateau Hough" from the fruit of those vines. Next to the vineyard is the open basement of a torn down Victorian home that Mansfield and others are capping with a glass roof, a "biocellar" as they call it, which will be used to grow food energy-efficiently year-round. The biocellar will be completed this summer, and the national urban farming community is going to be making its way to Cleveland to see if this groundbreaking re-use of abandoned inner city buildings can work.

As I walk up to Mansfield's front door, with the lawn edged to the concrete walk with geometric precision, trees and shrubs in symmetry from their orderly red mulch mounds, two-car garage out back, I keep thinking that this is suburbia. But then you think about how people from Eastlake and Avon and Brunswick perceive neighborhoods like this, places they've never been to but know them as a place where "those people" live, a place that a fairly high percentage of the white folks in Greater Cleveland consider a crime-ridden shithole ghetto where you wouldn't even drive through *with the car doors locked.* Getting out and walking around definitely isn't considered, even if someone is growing grapes.

And when Mansfield Frazier lets me in, his two dogs jumping and sniffing as good dogs do, we move through the vaulted-ceiling living room, past a beautiful open kitchen and his office with African art on the walls, to the back patio where we sit in the afternoon sun, on comfortable furniture in a fenced-in yard with a vegetable garden. No noise, no evidence that we might be in a high-crime area, just peace and quiet, like being 20 miles east or west or south.

Mansfield Frazier, 71, is a writer and builder and now a winemaker among other things, and he loves gardening and landscaping and home improvement projects, no different from most folks I know in that age group. So again, I catch myself in thinking of why this all surprises me. And then it hits me. Mansfield Frazier is not doing what he is supposed to do. Namely, people like him are expected to get away from E. 66th and Hough and ride out the back nine in some quiet place without much meaning, certainly without people yelling nonsense from their windows.

He then tells me he lives in Hough to make a point. In July 1966, just about a half-mile east of his homestead, what became known as the Hough Riots started and festered for about a week. It started when a black guy went into a bar at E. 79th and Hough, bought a bottle of wine, then asked for a glass of water on a day when the mercury hit 90. The white bar owner refused the request for the water, and then put a sign on his building that said "No Water for Niggers." That sign busted open the racial tension cork. After seven days of looting and shooting and firebombing, along with the Cleveland police and national guard troops cracking heads, four were dead and 30 critically injured.

So his quiet suburbia is here, where he likes it to be, where the lawns are beautiful and the dogs sniff and jump around and the vegetables grow in the back yard, and that nuisance shit stays on the other side of the patio fence. And when he explains why he lives where he does, like most things with Mansfield Frazier, the answer is both pretty simple and pretty complicated.

"Black folks hear all their lives that in order to get ahead, in order to improve their lives, they should move next door to white people," Frazier says, glass of red wine in his hand. "But I've never heard that white folks can improve their lives if they move next door to blacks. So we have been told that we should move to Solon and then Bentleyville and further and further away from the city so that we can succeed and that has never made any sense to me."

"Changing housing segregation patterns mean nothing to me," he continues. "I am interested in job segregation patterns and changing those. You have to do those first because the housing patterns are meaningless unless you do."

"Desegregation has not worked because it takes two to desegregate and I don't see both races taking on the aspects of desegregation in equal proportion," Frazier says. "So I feel I can do just fine right here and improve my life and the community if that is how we are judged.

And if white folks want to move down to Hough to improve their lives by living next door to me, I'm all for that and would welcome them. But I've never heard whites say they can improve their lives by living next door to someone who has my skin color."

> *Blacks have to learn to live, and live comfortably, with racism. To fail to do so will continue to cause us great harm. For if we fail to acknowledge this fact of American culture, and the permanence of it, we will continue to become victims of the bitterness and rancor, which has, in the past, prevented us from reaching our goals. Racism is damaging enough, without our shooting ourselves in the foot by allowing it to make us bitter, too.*
> —From *Behind the Wall* by Mansfield Frazier
> (Paragon House, 1995)

Frazier wrote the book *From Behind the Wall* while he was serving a two-year prison sentence that ended in 1995. He was a credit card forger for more than two decades, getting arrested 15 times and convicted five times. In some respects, his criminal record and prison time could have been much worse.

He was born in 1943, and his father owned a popular bar in Cleveland, the King's Tavern and Grill at E. 31st St. and Scovill Ave. (now Community College Ave.) in what was back then the heart of Cleveland's black middle class community. His father cooked ribs on a 20-foot smoker, sold beer and wine in the bar and hard liquor illegally by the bottle at the house out back (they didn't have a license for hard liquor). The bar was a social center of the black middle-class, where you had ribs and a beer after work and where you bought your numbers and collected when you hit. It was a cornerstone of the community, and Frazier said he was raised "like middle-class royalty."

He graduated from East Technical High School in 1961, and went to work for the Cleveland Electric Illuminating Company as a welder and pipefitter soon after graduation. He thought he was moving up with the company, but in 1969 he was told he had moved up as far as he could because the whites in the shop wouldn't accept a black guy as a supervisor. He says now he came very close to "going postal," because his father had taught him how to shoot when he was seven and he had a thirty-ought-six rifle at home and was thinking about bringing it to work.

"I remember sitting in my basement oiling up that thirty-ought-six, and I had no escape plan; really, the only plan I had was to discharge the weapon and kill as many people as I could," he says matter-of-factly. But with his marriage failing, and with another woman coming into the picture, Frazier said he decided to drop his plans for a mass shooting, instead leaving Cleveland and "dropping out of society."

So he used the machinists skills CEI had taught him to forge credit cards (they were exploding on the scene at the time) and traveled across America. Over time the game played out like this: he'd get arrested for a small charge, get a probation deal or short jail sentence, pay a small fine and/or turn over some of his equipment, and then get back in business. He explains it this way in his book: "I adopted my very strict code of ethics. I would never commit a crime against a person—I have never physically harmed anyone or taken anything from an individual. I always specialized in swindling institutions, what I term 'victimless' crime."

But while serving the two-year sentence at a federal prison in Kentucky in the mid-1990s, he decided to use the time to work on becoming a published writer. He devoured Shakespeare and other classic literature, kept up with newspaper columnists and studied their styles, and wrote a 750-word editorial every day. One of his mentors was Billy the Mad Bomber, who was doing 40 years for blowing up his partner's business and who had a master's in English. "Writing is a craft and if you have half a brain you can do it if you commit to working hard at it," he says.

His collection of essays eventually got published by Paragon House. He got out in 1995 and made a living from writing. He ghost-wrote books for businessmen, became a journalist for some of the free alt-weeklies like *The Tab* and *Cleveland Free Times*, and the *Cleveland Leader* and *Cool Cleveland*. Noted editor Tina Brown tapped him to be a contributor to the Daily Beast (he does less work for them now that she has left).

Along the way, he used his earnings to build his home and to consult with builders who were getting into the Hough revitalization of the late 1990s. Frazier knew about building from a practical construction standpoint, but he also knew how to get the right permits and push things through at city hall.

Charles Michener, a Cleveland native and former *New Yorker* editor who moved back to his hometown several years ago, helped hook up Frazier with Tina Brown and says Frazier's talent is more appreciated elsewhere than in Cleveland. For example, in reading Frazier's work, I immediately thought his style of writing would make him an ideal columnist for the *Plain Dealer*. "If he were white, maybe," Michener says. "[Newspapers] tend to shy away from risk taking these days and don't want to rock the boat, and a guy like Mansfield is going to stick out."

"He is very smart and is very much a community-minded person," Michener says. "But he doesn't just fall on the side of the blacks on everything. He blasts Obama on certain things, and the Cleveland black leadership as well. He is very open and honest about very difficult issues, but he never makes you feel uncomfortable when you talk about those things. He's one of the smartest people I've ever met."

So you might think Mansfield Frazier was content being a writer, a consultant on the incarcerated re-entering society, an advisor on real estate developments in Hough and other inner-city neighborhoods, and the owner of a fine home two miles from downtown and two miles from the Cleveland Clinic main campus. Happily married to Brenda for 16 years, and happy to ride his Harley-Davidson motorcycle on the weekends.

But he had some grapes growing in his backyard a few years ago and thought it might be a good idea to grow more of them across the street.

Frazier is dressed in his usual garb on this early May morning—overalls and work boots and a sweatshirt and a baseball cap—while he putters around on gravel between the vineyard and the biocellar project. He has hired guys recently out of prison from a halfway house nearby, and is very hands-on as he shows them how to do things like planing boards and chopping wood from a fallen tree and tuck-pointing some of the stones in the biocellar's foundation.

Things are moving along smoothly; some green leaves and buds are finally appearing on the vines after the record frigid winter, and volunteers had just helped fill up about 2,000 bottles with the first harvest (four years after the planting). A cistern to gather rainwater had been delivered a few days earlier, and is now sitting at the bottom of the nine-foot-deep basement that will be home to underground vegetable raising. But he needs to run over to Home Depot in the Steelyard Commons for some screws, metal angle brackets, and boards to build a staircase into the biocellar. He asks me to ride along in his pickup truck so we can take care of some of the interview while he picks up the materials.

One of the first things you realize while sitting with Mansfield Frazier is that he is very smart and has interests that are as diverse as almost anyone. He been doing a call-in radio show on Sunday nights at WTAM-AM 1100 for about a year, and he enjoys the public interaction. His topics can be all over the place, as evidenced on a recent show: he laid into Obama for his handling of the Veteran's Administration scandal, discussed the pros and cons of raising the minimum wage, and gave personal insight on the financial practicality of rehabbing old buildings in the inner city. He even gave home improvement advice on how to remove nails from wooden boards before sanding to keep the metal disc from being damaged.

"When we started the radio show, we got lots of texts and calls from listeners that they were going to get the program director to fire me, but that's pretty much stopped," he says. "I'm not going anywhere."

As for the plans for the winery and various applications of urban farming projects, Frazier explains how they must complement each other and have financial sustainability. "What we are looking at is the highest and best use for the land," he says. "I was growing grapes in my garden at home and joked to someone that we should make wine in Hough. It took off from there."

He was able to get the foreclosed ¾ acre plot that hosts the vines in 2010 for free through the Cuyahoga County Land Bank, and received a $15,000 grant from Re-Imagining Cleveland, a non-profit that works with the City of Cleveland and neighborhood organizations to help fund projects that develop land reuse in urban core areas. The vineyard is comprised of about 300 vines; half Frontenac, half Traminette, both cold-weather hardy varieties of winemaking grapes.

"I see urban farming as being an economic engine and a job creator," Frazier says. "There are huge swaths of land on the east side where new homes are not going to be built. So what do you do with that land? Urban agriculture makes sense, because we can solve the problem of land re-use and encourage healthy eating at the same time."

The biocellar idea came about when the Kent State University's Cleveland Urban Design Collaborative, which helped on gaining the original grant for the vineyard, visited the vineyard in 2011 and noticed a dilapidated house next door. Terry Schwarz, director of the KSU organization, had been working with Jean Loria, a Cleveland biologist who

141

wanted to explore tearing down houses and keeping basements intact for a greenhouse-type structure that could be used to grow food.

"We had known Mansfield from the vineyard project, and we were fascinated how quickly he had made the vineyard idea come to light, so we worked with him on the biocellar," Schwarz says.

There have been some biocellar-type projects built in Europe, but the one at E. 66th and Hough is believed to be the first of its kind in the United States. The idea is fairly simple: the frost line is at four feet in Ohio, and the basement floor on this house is nine feet below grade. The temperature will stay close to 55 degrees at that depth. Capping the basement with a solar energy glass greenhouse will enable food to be grown off the energy grid year-round. The costs of digging down past the frost line are taken out of the equation. Or so the thinking goes at this point.

The first crop might be shiitake mushrooms or something similar, a crop that does not need much water or sunlight so the bugs can be worked out regarding temperature variations and air circulation patterns and water redistribution collected from the glass roof.

Rob Donaldson, a local architect, designed the glass roof and admits that there are some growing pains with the initial design. "This is the first one, so we understand that as we do more of these we will find the efficiencies and be able to make it work better and cheaper," Donaldson says. "But we have already heard from organizations in other cities that are following this closely, because this is a simple and basic way to re-use abandoned property in a way that is sustainable and profitable investment for communities."

The Cleveland biocellar is about 500 square feet, and Donaldson thinks varied sizes could be used for different purposes. Smaller ones could be used for office space, larger ones could be used for housing with very cheap energy costs, perhaps completely off the grid.

Schwarz wonders if the cost structure for the biocellar is workable. The demolition of the above ground part of the house, combined with the new greenhouse top and plumbing and heating and air circulation infrastructure, could push the costs above $100,000. It would help if a number of biocellar structures could be constructed next to one another, Schwarz says, but that would require that six homes slated for teardown would be on the same block in close proximity to one another. "There is a lot of uncertainty if this is economically feasible for the long term according to our research," she says. "The question is how many years would it take to be profitable. No one really knows right now."

Frazier's goal is a mix between crop-growing and visitors. A winery could have tastings, and the busloads of visitors could tour the biocellar and perhaps greenhouses and community gardens and fish-raising pools close by. Before they get back on their bus, they might buy bottles of wine and bags full of shiitake mushrooms and tilapia.

But the prospect of a destination winery next to the vineyard has its unique set of problems. Strict federal and state regulations passed after Prohibition make it difficult to start making wine without a stand-alone building, owned by the winemaker, and all sorts of exact equipment. Frazier has an old library building next door to the vineyard in mind as a bottling plant and visitor center, but the cost of all the equipment and teardown of parts of the old structure could run to $500,000.

How to get that half mill? A combination of public and private money, and what he calls "angel investors." Those would be private foundations and philanthropists who would see the winery and biocellar grouping as a good investment for the community, and their interest in profits would not be as intense as regular Wall Street greedhead banks.

"One of the banks I've talked to wants to invest in the winery, but the first thing they told me was that I would have to fence off the vineyard from the neighborhood," he says. "I'm not going to do that, because this only works if the neighborhood perceives this as being a part of the community. But we'll work it out. We'll do some fundraising and get people on board. And I'll do what I always do. I'll find the smart experts who will tell me how to work around things like this."

"But I am completely confident we will get this done," he says.

While we're in the Home Depot, Frazier is trying to figure out how to get things done quickly with a reporter in tow. He assesses very quickly that he cannot send me to another aisle to get the right angle brackets or wood screws because I have no concept of what those things are. He figures I'll be best used to load up lumber and push the cart while he checks things off the list. "Just follow me," he says.

When Frazier needed someone who knew about growing grapes, he sought out Giancarlo Calicchia, an Italian painter and sculptor who also grows grapes for wine in Madison in Lake County east of Cleveland. Calicchia, 68, is also part owner of the Dante restaurant in Tremont and five other associated eateries in Northeast Ohio.

Callicchia has become fast friends with Frazier, maybe because of the closeness of their age, maybe because they have an artistic common ground, maybe because they share diverse interests. "I started out cutting stone for kitchen counters, and I always wanted to do sculpting and painting and I do that too," he says. "What I like about Mansfield is that he has created his own world, and he has dealt with his past and learned from it. He is a survivor, but also a very smart and practical survivor."

"What I have noticed most about him is that he comes from a past where he was treated in an abusive way, but I never see in him wanting to treat anyone is an abusive way to get back at them," Callicchia says. "He is always reinventing himself."

Back at the peaceful patio on Hough, talk once again turns to the local environs and what beckons for a city that seems to be having a difficult time digging itself out of the hole it currently finds itself in. That hole being population and job loss, high poverty rates, bad schools and race dislike and distrust that sometime borders on absurd. Just the usual.

But we find we are in agreement on one major point: while the Cleveland powers that be always like to blame outside forces for the deep holes it has found itself in through the years, we know that Cleveland is very adept at digging those holes on its own. The people here have been doing it for years.

And when we get back to the issue of race, it is quite apparent that Mansfield Frazier does not solely define himself by the issue, but does not hide from or try to sugarcoat it either. He has dealt with it his whole life, thinks Cleveland is more racist than most cities, and he knows when to not participate, "because I don't play the game when the game is rigged."

And if there is one part of the current racial makeup of Cleveland that bugs him, it is when whites think that things are equal now and the past doesn't matter anymore. In fact, he has a problem on both those assertions.

"If you put a knife in my back nine inches, and then pull it out six inches, don't say how great things are because that knife is still three inches deep in my back," Frazier says. "I don't care how you feel about me, just get the knife out of my back."

"Racism is a function of power and black racism cannot exist under the current power structure," he continues. "If I point out the fact that you are a racist, people have said I'm a racist for doing it. They say I am an uppity Negro because I will point out your wrongdoings. But the fact is that whites started it all by bringing us here, they perpetuated it, and when we call them on it, they say we are racists?"

And it is hard not to see his point. His grandmother was born a slave in 1860, and she was freed by the Emancipation Proclamation and this wasn't ancient history to him, because he knew her and talked to her and she died when he was 13. And he was there in 1966 when the world blew up in Cleveland because a white bar owner didn't think niggers should have a glass of water on a hot day. And, of course, he heard his bosses tell him that the whites in the shop weren't ready for a black supervisor so he should just keep quiet and bide his time and not get uppity over it.

So, that's that. But Mansfield did put a lot of it in perspective. And with a sense of humor about it all. "Stupid people are more prejudiced and all the data says we have a lower educational attainment here than in a lot of cities," he says. "Maybe we're just dumber here. Maybe we are just plain stupid."

But Mansfield is not stupid. He is able to see the changing landscape in Cleveland—both figuratively and literally—and how this big and probably last project for him has a chance to have a lasting impact on the neighborhood. Two blocks away, the city of Cleveland is spending more than $6 million restoring League Park—home of the Cleveland Indians from the 1890s until mid-1940—and the new sports and recreation center is scheduled to open in July. The health care industry is growing from University Circle west toward downtown, with biotech industries starting to be planted along Euclid Avenue.

There has been recent news of possible new developments around E. 55th St. and St. Clair Ave., which could push south toward the vineyard. Asiatown along Payne Ave. is solidifying. And Gust Gallucci's Italian market and classic lunch deli has been bringing the crowds from the city and suburbs to E. 66th St. and Euclid Ave. since it moved there in 1988.

So Mansfield Frazier is betting on the current market and where he sees the future going in this part of Cleveland. Because if suburbanites will flock to a historic Italian mainstay in the Cleveland urban core for their meatballs and prosciutto and olives for 25 years, maybe they will stop on down a few blocks away for some locally made wine and fresh vegetables, and cruise by a baseball field where Babe Ruth batted and

Bob Feller pitched. That's not crazy thinking.

Now the people who stop on down are probably not going to move in next door, at least not in the near future, but Mansfield Frazier figures those people will improve their lives through their experience in the inner city. And maybe improve the lives of those people who do live next door to him. That's not crazy thinking either.

V. Politics

The Secret History of Chief Wahoo

Brad Ricca

The recent decision by the U.S. Patent and Trademark Office to cancel the trademark registration of the Washington Redskins football team due to the "disparaging" nature of their name raises one question all over Cleveland: what about Wahoo?

Chief Wahoo, the logo of the Cleveland Indians, is kind of like Dracula. He has flashed his white teeth over the city for what seems like an eternity. Even as the team and Major League Baseball have quietly pushed the "block C" logo as the club's primary visual mark, Chief Wahoo still smiles from the uniform sleeves, caps, batting helmets, and stadium decor. Let's be honest: Could there ever be a Cleveland without Chief Wahoo? And I don't mean in terms of any eventual change in name or logo, but in the sheer amount of *stuff* that the Chief is already stitched in, ironed on, applied to, and inked in. In a town where you might spot a Couch, Edwards, or Frye jersey up at Applebee's on any given Thursday, Wahoo trumps all of them. Wahoo in Cleveland is like infrastructure: it is way down in the bowels of things. We have to follow it down to its dark source.

We know that the Chief is beloved—or offensive—for many, depending on who you ask. Weeks before this year's home opener, the *Cleveland Plain Dealer* called for the "racially insensitive" Wahoo to finally be retired. At the same time, local company GV Art & Design sold out of t-shirts emblazoned with "Keep the Chief." Chief Wahoo, in the battleground state of Ohio, still splits friends and family across all sorts of boundaries. Why? Because people disagree about what Wahoo really means.

In baseball, meaning comes down to history, whether it is numbers in a box score or stories shared over pretzels and beer. Even in the era of high-definition replay, history is the only thing we can agree on. For example: I can't stand the Yankees, but I can agree that Mariano Rivera was an all-time great closer (with some great entrance music). That's why we hate talking about changing baseball history so much when men asterisk themselves to get into the record books. We need a baseline .000 to create meaning. We hate when we are wrong about history.

So what if we are wrong about Wahoo?

It turns out that much—much—of what we think we know about Chief Wahoo is wrong. Even the origin of the name "Indians" is debated. The team's front office claims that the Indians name honors an old "full-blooded Native American" named Louis Sockalexis who played for the club in the late nineteenth century. Over a succession of franchises in multiple leagues, Cleveland baseball clubs couldn't stick on a nickname. Perhaps the worst was the old Players' League franchise, the Infants, who lost 75 of the 130 games in their lone season. In 1901, Cleveland's franchise in the new American League was called the Blues, then the Bronchos in 1902. The team settled on the Naps in 1903 after Napoleon Lajoie, the future Hall-of-Famer second baseman. But when Nap left after the 1914 season, the team needed a new hero—and a new name.

On January 18, 1915, a *Plain Dealer* article titled "Looking Backward," confirms that "many years ago there was an Indian named Sockalexis who was the star player … the team will be named 'Indians' to honor him." But many current writers and historians call foul. Ellen J. Staurowsky first suggested in a landmark 1998 article that the new name may have been piggybacking on the popularity of the 1914 Boston Braves, who miraculously rose from worst to first in mid-season. Craig Calcaterra of NBC's *Hardball Talk* agrees, calling the Sockalexis story "bogus." Keith Olbermann just calls it "lies." The Braves angle passes the common-sense test: Borrowing the ideas of a successful team is a tradition as old as the game itself. Picking "Indians" to evoke "Braves" seems very plausible, especially when you consider baseball's love of superstition. What could be better karma than adopting a nickname inspired by the team that just won it all?

Still, other accounts support the idea that the name actually is meant to honor Sockalexis, who was, from May to July 1897, a very good baseball player. In fact, Sockalexis was so beloved—he was hitting over .370 that spring—that the sportswriters wrote poems to him in the newspaper. In the *Plain Dealer*:

> *This is bounding Sockalexis*
> *Fielder of the mighty Clevelands*
> *All the crowd cries: "Sockalexis,*
> *Sockalexis, Sockalexis!"*
> *When he circles like the eagle*
> *Round the bases, or serenely*
> *Slides upon his solferine*
> *Pie and doughnut padded stomach,*
> *Wiping all the glaring war paint*
> *Off his nasal in a jiffy.*

SOCKALEXIS BREAKING FOR THIRD.

There is an old tone at work here. The focus of the "poem" on his war paint, belly, and nose uses praise for his play as an excuse for casual racism. They didn't even need cartoons in 1897. During Sockalexis' magic May, the paper riffed on the infamous words of General Philip Sheridan, stating "The man who said that there are no good Indians except dead Indians ... surely never saw one Louis Sockalexis."

Turn-of-the-century sportswriters really wrote like that. Even when they clap, they get in their digs. On May 6, 1897, in a loss against Cincinnati, "the greatest portion of the glory in yesterday's game fell to the lot of Sockalexis," who scored a homerun and cut off a runner at the plate in "a sensational fielding play ... that will not be soon forgotten." The writer calls Sockalexis "Big-Man-Not-Afraid-of-His-Job." Was this racism, or just the way people thought back then? Does it matter?

By June, Sockalexis was so popular that local ads started using his name to endorse their products, almost certainly without his approval.

In ads, John, Browning, King & Co. brag that their wares are "going at prices that astonish even Sokalexis."

But few ballplayers can play a perfect summer. By July, things took a turn for Sockalexis. In a recap from July 8, 1897 titled "A Wooden Indian," Sockalexis "played very much like one for once" as he struggled at the plate. Finally, by August 17, the paper reveals that the ailing Sockalexis has been "under suspension for some time because of his too infrequent indulgence in the flowing bowl." There was even fear of a leg amputation due to "blood poisoning," among other scandalous rumors.

Sockalexis' reversal of fortune due to his struggles with alcoholism—and his subsequent treatment by the press—was so absolute that even the national papers got involved. On October 19, the Baltimore News ran a three-chapter opus titled "The Song of Sockalexis:"

> *All your wampum couldn't*
> *Coax me from the cup that cheers me ...*
> *I'd rather play a date with Booze than anything I know of!*
> *Thus departed Sockalexis*
> *To the Land of Awful Headaches,*
> *To the daffy land of Dopedum*
> *And the forests, dark and lonely*

Sockalexis died on Christmas Eve 1913 at the age of 42 on an Indian reservation in Maine. The *Plain Dealer* called Sockalexis "the greatest natural baseball player that ever lived." But they go on:

Flattery and homage turned the head of the aborigine: he fell into bad habits and became utterly beyond the reach of discipline. "He was only an Indian, after all," commented the enthusiasts who had been his most eager admirers.

No baseball player should be immune to the barbs of his hometown press box. But Sockalexis was treated differently because of his race, even when he was great, and especially when he was bad. When Cleveland's sportswriters were polled in 1915 to pick a new name for the team, did they honor Sockalexis out of nostalgia for an exciting couple of months of play—or was it out of guilt for the way they treated him? Or was it a crack—like "Infants"—at a horrible last-place team? Sockalexis was a failed prospect whose tragedy was, in the words of the papers, inseparable from his heritage. Still, his very presence in the majors was and is still—and I think rightfully so—seen by many as heroic. In *Louis Sockalexis: The First Cleveland Indian,* David L. Fleitz calls him "the Native American version of Jackie Robinson."

The official origin of the Wahoo logo seems much less problematic. The accepted story goes that in 1947, half a century after Sockalexis, Indians owner Bill Veeck hired a kid named Walter Goldbach, 17, who designed the caricature. Goldbach, who worked for a local ad agency, defends Wahoo to this day. He explains that "it was the last thing on my mind [to] offend someone." After some alterations in 1951 (less nose, more red), the Wahoo image became the version we see today, though in greatly reduced use on the official uniform and around Progressive Field.

But that's not the real origin of the famous Wahoo cartoon.

The truth is that a very similar caricature was already in heavy unofficial use for fifteen years before Veeck commissioned Wahoo in 1947. On May 3, 1932, this small image appeared on the front page of the *Plain Dealer:*

The victory left the Indians one game behind Washington, the first place team.
Full Details on Today's Sport Pages.

There is a long history of racial stereotyping in cartoons depicting Native Americans, making many of them, by definition, similar in appearance. That's part of the problem. Still, this looks a lot like our Wahoo. The next day:

ST. LOUIS .... 0 1 0 4 0 4 0 1 1—11 .
CLEVELAND .... 1 0 4 0 0 1 1 0 1— 8

Full Details on Today's Sport Pages.

Readers liked the cartoon, so it continued, through bad games and rainouts:

The character came to be called "The Little Indian." He poked his head out on every front page to relay the previous game's outcome. He became a visual box score that anyone, including kids, could read.

The creator of the Little Indian was native Clevelander Fred George Reinert, who came up with the image soon after being hired in the early thirties. He became so popular that "Whenever school children toured the *Plain Dealer* office, they almost always asked to see the man who drew 'the little Indian.'"

"Good old Reiny" drew many sports cartoons before retiring in 1962. He then went into business with his son, worked in local television, and drew official caricatures for the Pro Football Hall of Fame. Even after his retirement, the paper covered his activities and urged fans to write him letters when he was ill.

The Little Indian ran for thirty years. The similarities to the modern-day Wahoo, which it predated by fifteen years, are astounding.

A friend of Reinert's named George Condon noted in a 1972 column that "When the baseball club decided to adopt an Indian car-

The Plain Dealer

Fred G. Reinert
1962 Photograph

icature as its official symbol, it hired an artist to draw a little guy who came very close to Reinert's creation; a bloodbrother, unquestionably."

Condon seems to be the only one who ever said this, at least in print. When Reinert died in 1974, he was a Cleveland sports fixture. Yet he is not named in any official Indians literature, or in any books about the creation of the Wahoo logo.

But what about the actual name of "Chief Wahoo?" No one can seem to pinpoint when it first appeared. Reinert didn't come up with it. "When I first created him," he said in a later interview, "I had picked out the name of Tommy Hawk, but then I found out somebody else had thought of the name first." Goldbach didn't, either. He says that the name is inaccurate: "He's a brave, he says. He only has one feather. Chiefs have full headdresses." So who named Chief Wahoo?

"Chief Wahoo" was actually a fairly common nickname for any generic Indian character. In fact, there was a popular newspaper comic strip called "Big Chief Wahoo" that ran from 1936 to 1947. The main character, a naïve, helpful fellow, looks little like the Indians' Wahoo image, but the name may have been influential. "Wahoo" was also a popular baseball cheer in Cleveland. Peter Pattakos, in his 2012 Scene article "The Curse of Chief Wahoo," notes that boosters were hand-fed "New Rooting Lingo for the Fans," including the bizarre, Chewbacca-like "WAHOO ZOEA-ERK!" when the new name was announced in 1915.

The Little Indian's similarities to the modern-day Wahoo are astounding.

In the press, the name "Chief Wahoo" doesn't seem to appear until 1950. Wahoo's debut in official accounts offers a tantalizing possibility of not only where the name might have come from, but who Tribe fans associated it with.

In the *Plain Dealer* on June 22, 1942, fans are urged to "Remember the name of Allie Reynolds ... He's a real Indian and unless the signs

158

are all wrong he'll be a Cleveland Indian ... he recently struck out 37 batters in three consecutive games" in the minors. On August 2 of that same year: "Of all their minor league prospects, the Indians feel most optimistic about a pitcher named Allie Reynolds."

When Reynolds—a member of the Muscogee (Creek) Nation—finally makes it to Cleveland as a September call-up in 1942, he was described as "swarthy, black-eyed Allie Reynolds" in an introductory spread in the paper. He is portrayed as a family man whose lifelong dream was simply "to be a pitcher."

Allie Reynolds pitched in his first major league game on September 17, 1942 and made two more relief appearances that season. When next spring rolled around, Reynolds was designated an "Unsigned Tribesman" and was uncertain to even make the team. But he earned a bullpen gig with the 1943 club. His early, impressive strikeout totals (151 by season's end to lead the AL), soon snagged him a starting job.

Reynolds pitched for the Indians for five years, mostly as a starter. He worked in 139 games and finished a quarter of them. With Bob Feller serving in the armed forces (Reynolds, as a father, was exempt), Allie became a fan favorite.

On October 11, 1946, Reynolds was traded to the New York Yankees. Since Feller was untouchable, Yankee star Joe DiMaggio reportedly suggested his bosses to ask for Reynolds, because he could never hit the Cleveland pitcher's fastball. The Tribe got great second basemen Joe "Flash" Gordon in return.

Indians fans can guess what happened next. Reynolds was good with the Indians. He was great with the Yankees. He was a part of six World Series championships, five in a row from 1949 to 1953. He averaged almost 18 wins a season over his first six years. In the summer of 1951, he threw two no-hitters. Manager Casey Stengel said "Reynolds was two ways great, which was starting and relieving, which no one can do like him ... He has guts." In the postseason, Reynolds sparkled. In World Series play, he went 7–2 with a 2.79 ERA over 77 innings, including three Series-clinching performances in relief. In 26 postseason at-bats, he hit .308.

A surprising nickname for Reynolds' appears on October 6, 1950 in his old local paper, the *Plain Dealer*. Under the title of "Chief Wahoo Whizzing," Reynolds fans learn that "Allie (Chief Wahoo) Reynolds, the copper-skinned Creek" lost to Philadelphia, but "in the clutches, though, the Chief was a standup gent—tougher than Sitting Bull."

The Yankees are always big baseball news (even in Cleveland), but Reynolds especially garnered a lot of coverage in his old town. In subsequent articles, he is called "Chief Wahoo," "old Wahoo," and just plain "Wahoo."

Reynolds saved some of his best stuff for his old team. His first no-hitter in July of 1951 was against the Indians and Feller (his former roommate). In that game, "Chief Wahoo" retired the final seventeen Indians batters. In New York, writers called Reynolds "Super Chief," probably after a popular high-speed train. But it was perhaps a natural extension of his previous Cleveland nickname. But "Super Chief" stuck, and that nickname is inscribed on Reynolds' gold plaque in Yankee Stadium. Reynolds was one of the first former Indians to make a difference on successful Yankees squads, a club that includes Graig Nettles, David Justice, and C.C. Sabathia. Reynolds started a fruitful relationship between the two teams, you could say. Or a curse, depending on what city you live in.

The name "Chief Wahoo" also appeared in the popular Cleveland sports column "The Sports Trail" by Jimmy Doyle. On May 25, 1951, Doyle writes that "It's great to see Bob Feller show how he's mastered that old pitching know how" and signs it "Chief Wahoo's-this" as a possible parting shot against the departed Reynolds. The Wahoo's-this character (one of many employed in Doyle's writing), would hang around for a while, making pro-Indians statements, as if to say "What was that other guy's name again? You know, the one who keeps winning championships in New York?" The first time "Chief Wahoo" is given as the name for the Indians' physical mascot is in 1952, when a person in a Wahoo costume shows up for a kids' party at Public Hall given by "Cleveland's dentists." Was Wahoo ever mentioned before 1950? That is unclear. *The Plain Dealer*, the paper of record, doesn't mention the name until 1950, and then only as a nickname for Allie Reynolds.

Reynolds, despite a 131–60 record with the Yankees and some incredible postseason numbers, never made it to the Hall of Fame. He didn't mind. "Teamwork was more important than some kind of honor," he said. Reynolds died in 1994 in his native Oklahoma. His career, and his life, was the stuff of baseball legend. He thought being paid to play the game he loved "was the greatest thing in the world." His success as a Yankee must have been rage-inducing to Tribe fans.

§

What does Chief Wahoo mean? Is it "just" a logo or is it a scarlet letter on our collective golf shirts, symbolizing lots of history and people we don't really understand? With the exception of the Sockalexis story—maybe—Clevelanders don't know the story of the Little Indian, or Allie Reynold's nickname. I'll be totally honest: it wasn't that hard to find. So are we all that afraid of history?

Regardless of where individual Clevelanders stand on whether the image is offensive, we shouldn't argue with history, or use its omissions as an excuse. The nickname "Indians" and the image of Chief Wahoo are the product of a long lineage that includes a tragic player treated horribly by the press, a beloved local artist who never got the credit he deserved, and a superstar pitcher who was traded away—at the height of his powers—to the hated New York Yankees. If those aren't Cleveland things, then Cleveland things don't exist.

The true history of Wahoo might not be the best reason to consider a change in logo or name—or even a reason to consider change at all. The discussion about Wahoo is about more than just cartoons or nicknames. We all know that. But I can't imagine any Indians fan I know not being horrified—no, make that, grab-the-folding-chair livid—that their symbol is named after a guy who won six World Series championships for the Yankees.

And I lied a little about the first reference to "Chief Wahoo" in the Cleveland papers. If you look beyond baseball, the first appearance of the name really occurred on June 1, 1938 when "Chief Wahoo came in second ... in the fourth race of greyhounds at Bainbridge."

History in baseball is important, for so many reasons. But so is karma. If you believe in that sort of thing.

The Great Lakes: Plans for the Next 100 Years

Daniel J. McGraw

When *Phil Enquist talks about the Great Lakes,* he often jumps from being the serious, architectural engineering type to someone who is amazed how the lake can sometimes be moody and brooding before storms come in. He talks of the science of limiting phosphorus on farmland to keep algae blooms from exploding, but then wafts into a soliloquy about how the Great Lakes waves are calming and more rhythmic than those on ocean beaches.

Or about visual allure and harsh symbolism of the flames that belch out from the lips of the flare stacks at the steel mills, and the mountains of coal and taconite nearby. And the vast number of fish and wildlife and flora that share that space. And how rivers are often the natural feature that divides the land, while huge lakes like these inland seas tend to unite. But the 62-year-old who calls Chicago home always gets back to his main point, which he has been touting almost religiously for the past five years.

"Cities will be fighting over water in this century, and we as a nation and a planet have to figure out how we are going to deal with that," says Enquist. "And globalization is a big part of that. We are all connected, and what we do here will affect what others are doing around the world."

The Great Lakes are the largest freshwater concentration on the planet; 20 percent of the world's water supply and 85 percent of the surface water in North America. There's about 295,000 square miles of land in the watershed and 11,000 miles of coastline. That's about twice as much waterfront here in the Midwest than there is ocean coastline in the entire continental United States. And here is one statistic that shows just how much water we are talking about: If you took all the water from the Great Lakes and spread it over the entire continental United States, the entire country would be under ten feet of water.

Enquist, as a highly recognized urban planning architect with Skidmore, Owings and Merrill (SOM) in Chicago, is known around the globe as a guy who specializes in planning for emerging cities and global migration. He chairs and fellows lots of academic institutions and planning organizations. His work takes him from the Bohai Bay Rim in China to Bahrain to an abandoned industrial wasteland on the south side of Chicago where the Calumet River flows into Lake Michigan and what was once a 600-acre steel mill is being converted into a community of 30,000 residents.

Water and its relationship to a new urbanism is at the core of what Enquist does. Talking with him about the interconnected big five inland seas, he blends in all the evils of Asian carp, the water shortages the world faces, the history of industrial pollution in our backyard, and the impact of climate change. Plus carbon footprints and high density and renewable energy thrown in for good measure.

About five years ago, SOM decided to provide a free planning initiative headed by Enquist called The Great Lakes Century. Inspired by famed Chicago architect Daniel Burnham, who drew up masterful urban plans for Cleveland and Chicago and other cities pro bono more than 100 years ago, Enquist and his colleagues want to partly disengage the political and jurisdictional boundaries of all the government entities that border the lakes and get them thinking about common goals. And long-term rather than short-term planning.

From a practical standpoint, getting two countries and eight states and two provinces and hundreds of counties and 10,000-plus cities to have common goals and think of them in terms of 100 years instead of next week goes against of lot of human nature. And it's not like this hasn't been tried before. Plenty of commissions and agencies and overlapping academic and economic clusters have been part of Great Lakes planning for hundreds of years.

But Enquist gets a bit excited when talking about that side of the equation. "We aren't talking about some utopian fantasy here," he said. "The Great Lakes basin is unique and we are at a time in history when people can live and interact in ways that are unique. We have probably the most valuable resource on the planet, and we mostly have ignored its well-being for more than 100 years."

"What we have done throughout those hundred years is to develop our cities with their backs to the lakes," he continued. "If we change that attitude and develop our living areas where we face and interact with the lakes, a lot on interesting changes will come about."

So we should face the toilet, instead of turning our back to the toilet, I suggest in a half-joking way.

"Yes, we have to face the toilet," Enquist laughed. "Because those lakes are our toilet, but they are also our source of drinking water and commerce and transportation and agriculture and so many other things. So often, our political leadership haven't understood that basic point, that the lakes are involved in almost everything in this part of the country. This part of the country should be the focal point of the United States and Canada in so many areas right now, but we need to change how we think about the Great Lakes. That's what we are trying to do."

§

I wasn't completely joking about the toilet reference, because I heard that from my father many times. I grew up a few houses from the Lake Erie shoreline on the east side of Cleveland, and when we were kids in the 1960s, my Dad would advise us that swimming should be done in pools and not in toilets. He was born in 1930 and for his generation, who grew up in Cleveland away from the shoreline, Lake Erie was the community toilet. It was where you put your factories and railroad lines and highways and other things people didn't want to live near. Because steel mills and coal burning electric plants functioned well near toilets, people not so much.

My Mom, on the other hand, grew up right on Lake Erie and she saw it in a more communal way. She would throw us in the water when we were six months old or so, and let the waves wash us back to shore. When we went to Euclid Beach Park, we rode the Thriller and looked at the scary Laughing Sal, but she also made sure we brought our swimsuits. And we combed the beaches for the rounded glass pebbles, wondered where that glass came from, and looked out on the horizon at the ore carriers that came from places we could find on the globe. For her, Lake Erie had an important sense of place.

But I still have one memory from my youth that clearly defines in my mind what Lake Erie was like back then. We lived just east of the Cleveland sewage treatment plant, and as I stood on a small concrete pier near our house one day at age seven, there were turds and toilet paper floating in the lake. The water was the color of coffee with cream. There was a sheepshead fish floating on its back next to the pier with a dark lamprey sucking out its guts. There was a bad smell in the air.

So I had general pollution and fecal matter and garbage fish and an invasive species and stink all rolled up in one imprint on my brain representing Lake Erie.

I mentioned my fond Lake Erie memory to Ohio U.S. Rep. Marcy Kaptur, who first got elected in 1982 and grew up in Toledo. "People have to remember that Lake Erie and the other Great Lakes were much worse back then, so we have made some progress," she said. "But we still have so much more work to do, and the first on that list is getting the country to realize what we have here."

Kaptur can run down a litany of issues she had to deal with in her 34 years in Congress: Getting the Great Lakes Restoration Initiative up and running in 2010, and then fighting year after year for about $300 million of annual cleanup funding; working with a US and Canadian joint commission to reduce by 50 percent the phosphorus fertilizer run-off from farms that has caused big algae blooms in western Lake Erie; getting slag heaps near the Black River in Elyria cleaned up after a steel mill closed; even working with Ohio tourism officials to find better access for bird watchers at the 6,700-acre Ottawa National Wildlife Refuge on the lakeshore just east of Toledo.

But when you get Kaptur to step back from the minutia for a minute, she says there is one big problem in Washington when it comes to the Great Lakes. "They really have no concept of basic geography, you know, basic stuff that we learned in elementary school," she said. "And I'm talking about Republicans and Democrats."

What the Democrat is talking about are the federal subsidies that have created farms and large cities out of deserts that we are still paying for. The Bureau of Reclamation goes back about 100 years, but began its huge influence in the 1930s with Depression-era spending on dams and reservoirs that make the bureau the largest wholesaler of water in the nation and the second largest producer of hydroelectric power, with 58 plants. It does this with about 250 dams and 350 reservoirs, which are used for power, irrigation, flood control, and recreation.

All that costs taxpayers about $2 billion a year in subsidies for electricity and water, with most of it going to agricultural interests. For Kaptur, the subsidies need to be scaled back over time, based upon the fact that growing tomatoes in the desert doesn't make much sense anymore.

"A tomato travels between 1,200 and 1,500 miles to get from the farm to the household table in the United States," she said. "Now we have some of the most fertile land on earth here in Ohio, and we have the water that we can bring to farms cheaply and efficiently. But our national policy is to subsidize the farmers growing in a desert to such an extent that farmers in the Midwest have little chance to compete."

"But once again, the point we are trying to make in Washington is that the Great Lakes basin is one of the only self-sustaining regions on the planet," Kaptur said. "We have water, we have fertile soil, we have shipping for transportation that supports manufacturing, we have recreation opportunities, and we have our own unique energy sources. We should be investing more right here."

"Doesn't that make sense?" she asked.

Ohio Sen. Sherrod Brown echoed Kaptur's take on the subsidies and told Belt: "It is not just subsidies for agriculture, it is subsidies for golf courses and swimming pools that we are all paying for. Clearly there is a reason that so much industry and growth and educational innovation took place around the Great Lakes through the years, but federal policy has turned its back on that in favor of growth in the west and the south."

And that is the major problem of future investment in the Great Lakes. The subsidies that the Midwest legislators helped approve throughout most of the 20th century led to population growth in the western and southern states and diminished power in the Midwest. And members of Congress aren't going to easily give back those appropriations that have been a part of their states' basic services for so long. And the western legislators will also ignore droughts that show that too much land is being farmed and wildfires that destroy homes in the mountains that could never have been built without grants for infrastructure.

Barry Rabe, a professor of environmental policy and the director of the Center for Local, State, and Urban Policy (CLOSUP) at the Gerald R. Ford School of Public Policy at the University of Michigan, said the declining population in states like Michigan and Ohio make it difficult to reverse some of the billions of dollars in federal subsidies to which Rep. Kaptur and Sen. Brown allude.

"We all know that the ones who scream the most about budget deficits are from the states in the south and west that receive these huge grants for programs that subsidize their ability to live there," Rabe said. "But a number of factors can come into play. Increased drought from climate change might make Washington look closer at the Great Lakes region. Having the shale gas here and wind farms on the lakes—along with an inexhaustible supply of cheap water—may make some investment companies look at this area differently."

"I don't think anyone or any business is just going to pick up and move to Detroit or Cleveland because they are on a large body of water," Rabe said. "But if that body of water is clean and provides great parks and recreation for employees of a company, and if there are energy efficiencies that a company can't get elsewhere, and it can tap into areas of expertise the Midwest has in manufacturing, then yes, the location is a big issue."

"But it isn't going to happen unless the different states join up in better ways to work together," Rabe said. "That's the bigger issue."

§

John Norquist was the mayor of Milwaukee from 1988 to 2004 and now serves as the CEO and President of the Congress of New Urbanism (CNU), a collection of urban planners and architects who promote functional urban design in buildings and neighborhoods. When asked about his relationship with the State of Wisconsin during his time as Milwaukee mayor, Norquist said, "Milwaukee was like an albatross around Madison's neck."

Norquist said that that attitude came about because of the lack of understanding of the needs of a city on the water and the needs on those living in the interior. "It is really basic stuff," Norquist said. "People who live in agricultural areas want things spread out and they fight congestion. They don't want anything close together."

"But cities, especially along the water, need to be concentrated around that port area. All of the state capitals in the Midwest are away from the lakes, and the state governments always spend money and time trying to spread the cities out."

"[State officials'] goals were always to spread things out, because that is what they knew," he continued. "I had to deal with it in Milwaukee and they dealt with it in Detroit and Cleveland. Rather than invest in the areas closest to the water, they engaged in policies and spending that moved everyone and everything away from the water. The problem is that the State of Ohio applies a rural standard to Cleveland, and that's why Cleveland is the way it is."

Cuyahoga County Executive Ed FitzGerald, who is running for Ohio governor, said he has seen some of those same state policies while in his current post and when he was mayor of Lakewood. "There really has always been a lack of focus out of Columbus," FitzGerald said. "While I served on city council and as mayor of Lakewood [1999-2011], the state rarely engaged us on any issue where being on Lake Erie came into play. Certainly not in planning where we would meet with leaders of other cities nearby to have a regional approach."

"Lake Erie is part of an economic engine that crosses all boundaries and part of a Great Lakes region where the eight states and Canada have common interests," FitzGerald said. "A lot of elected officials say they all want clean water and energy efficiencies and sustainable development and job growth, but you need to do something about it and not just talk. Our governor isn't doing much to really use this precious and unique resource to make an impact. I don't think he really tries to understand the issues at play."

Ohio Gov. John Kasich did not respond to repeated requests for an interview for this story.

§

If cities are supposed to turn toward and not away from their lakefront, it will be interesting to see what Cleveland will do in coming years. Chicago has always had extensive parks along Lake Shore Drive, and Detroit has grown the Detroit River International Wildlife Refuge from 300 acres in 2001 to about 6,000 today, with possible plans for another 10,000 acres. Under Norquist's leadership, Milwaukee tore down a freeway downtown to better connect the downtown urban neighborhood to Lake Michigan.

Under FitzGerald, the county is working with the city on developing a small property just north of the Cleveland Browns Stadium. FitzGerald also met with "Lake Erie stakeholders" last fall—representatives from the fishing industry, manufacturers, shippers, and others—to get their views on water issues. The county now has an online page that will provide the latest news on subjects like invasive species, how much debris is removed from the lake, fishing reports, and others.

But neither FitzGerald nor Sen. Brown wanted to get into any discussion regarding what the City should do with Burke Lakefront Airport. Both said it was a city issue, and it was up to Cleveland to do what they wished with the airport, which has about half the number of flights it did in 2000 and sits on 450 acres of prime lakefront property downtown. Cleveland Mayor Frank Jackson did not respond to requests for an interview for this story.

Kaptur, however, wants to discuss the options the city of Cleveland might have in developing better access to the lake. She said she has been encouraged by the transfer of Edgewater and the Euclid Beach parks from the state to the Cleveland MetroParks, and wants to see if she can help facilitate federal involvement in getting more public access to Lake Erie.

To that end, she has invited U.S. National Park Service Director Jonathan Jarvis to speak at the Cleveland City Club, after which Jarvis will attend meetings to explore extending the Cuyahoga Valley National Park to the lakefront in some way. Kaptur said examining whether Burke Lakefront Airport can be included in that park expansion, "will definitely be part of the discussion." She also said that "this is a tremendous opportunity, especially given that FirstEnergy is going to close its Lake Shore power plant just east of downtown, and Cleveland could have better lakefront access than most cities on the Great Lakes.

§

Of course, Enquist's planning group is big on more parks in their 100-year vision. They are suggesting in very vague terms that an international park operated by the United States and Canada be formed in the Great Lakes basin, though how they might acquire property is not yet spelled out and what role local governments might have in the process is too far down the road at this point.

There are the environmental issues that have to be sorted out, particularly the invasive species that have run the gamut from lampreys to zebra mussels to Asian carp through the years. "It is something that we really have to pay attention to and work hard at," said Jon Allan, who grew up in Elyria, Ohio, and is now director of the State of Michigan's Office of the Great Lakes. "Some of the invasive species could be benign, but others could suck the life out of the Great Lakes."

The Great Lakes Century also thinks a high-speed rail line running from Chicago to Toronto (in three hours' time) would be a good investment, providing a transportation option that would be quicker and less polluting than airplanes. And then there is the issue of passenger boat lines. A federal law called the Jones Act, passed in 1920, requires all ships operating between U.S. ports be owned by U.S. companies and have a completely American crew.

The freight shippers operating on the Great Lakes have lobbied hard to keep the antiquated act as federal law so that foreign competitors find it more difficult to operate in the Great Lakes, but Enquist and others think there might be a way to separate passenger service from the shipping regulations. "It is amazing the Jones Act is still on the books," said CNU's Norquist. "The fact that we have the largest freshwater inland lake system in the world and we have federal laws that make it pretty much impossible to ferry passengers around is just crazy."

And that is a perfect example on how difficult it will be to make significant changes in how the Great Lakes are used and improved. Most everyone agrees that there would be a market for cruise ships running from Toronto to Chicago, with stops in Buffalo and Cleveland and Detroit and other cities along the way. But that can't be done easily because freight shipping companies transporting iron ore between Duluth and Cleveland want to protect their business interests.

And one would think that the passenger and the ore shipping interests would be unrelated, but everything having to do with the Great Lakes is connected to other parts of the region. No one ever thought that some shellfish native to the Black Sea might one day affect the cost of producing electricity in Ohio, but they did and are still doing so 25 years later.

Enquist likes to point out that the Great Lakes basin on the U.S. side could easily handle an increase in population between 50 and 75 million by 2050, given the vacant property and water resources available. And he said that while the region experiences that growth, it can adapt new ways to reinvent itself.

"We used to just focus on carbon-based industries in the Great Lakes, but most of those have left or are leaving," Enquist said. "And part of the problem is that we have let governmental and jurisdictional boundaries get in the way of doing development and progressing in the right ways. We can reinvent our relationship with the lakes."

And maybe that's why The Great Lakes Century is opting for the 100-year plan. Because, to use a shipping reference, you can't turn the Queen Mary around on a dime. It will be difficult to get the federal government to stop dumping money into the desert so they can grow tomatoes, harder still to get away from the coal-fired power plants and into renewable energy, equally tough to move highways and railroads and factories away from the water, and probably impossible to get eight states and two countries and two provinces and thousands of local governments to agree upon these things.

But Congresswoman Marcy Kaptur is ever the optimist. "The federal government needs a course correction when it comes to the Great Lakes," she said. "We live in a most wonderful part of the earth and it is a part of the earth that produces. And we've proven that we can produce in a private market without those huge subsidies."

"Maybe we just need to teach the rest of the country about this," she laughed. "Maybe a little basic geography."

A Tale of Two Foreclosures

Laura Putre

During the height of the foreclosure crisis, more than 10,000 individuals and families across the city of Cleveland faced losing their homes in a single year. My home in suburban Lakewood, bought in 2010, was a foreclosure in 2007. Four of the ten homes nearest it, including the house next door, were foreclosures, too.

I moved in too late to know any of the people who lost their homes, so I just hear bits and pieces. They weren't all angels; who said they had to be? The former owner of my house, I'm told, lived with her grandchildren, a couple of hardened teens who tormented the neighbors. Next door, say the neighbors, was a woman so hated by her landlord, he decided to foreclose to remove her from the property.

The houses have new occupants now, kids and pets and their required adults. But even with all the action happening here, I feel like we're living with ghosts. Ten thousand-plus people—and that's just in one year—have to go somewhere, whether it's the next street over or a trailer park or to another state. During the foreclosure crisis, there were a lot of stories about people losing their homes; but now that they're gone, we hear very little about where they actually went. Are they living out their golden years in a small rental a few streets away from their home of 40 years, like a couple I know? Or maybe they've gone back to West Virginia to live with family they can't stand.

I wanted to see how hard it would be to find people who'd lost their homes to foreclosure, to track what happened to them. I wanted three, for contrast's sake. And they'd have to talk on the record.

It wouldn't be too hard, right? Everyone in Cleveland knew someone who'd lost a house, from their Aunt Phoebe to the displaced neighbor whose washing machine they bought for 50 bucks. And if word of mouth and the collective brain-wracking of Facebook friends failed, surely I'd find someone in the constellation of Cleveland social service agencies that dealt with foreclosure.

But this story became "A Tale of Two Foreclosures" (I think Dickens would approve) when, after a month of trying, I still couldn't find a third family who'd lost a home to foreclosure who would let me use their names and tell their story.

§

One of the people who did talk to me was Sheri West, a youthful grandmother who reads motivational books and likes to network in her spare time. West lost her home in 2008, the second-worst year of Cleveland's foreclosure crisis. I got in touch with her through LinkedIn, where her profile describes her as a "visionary entrepreneur," though for the time being she's working through an agency as a home caregiver for seniors.

The world has heard about West before. In 2009, when she was living at a shelter amid the houseplants she'd rescued from her former home, she was the subject of a *New York Times* article on a rise in foreclosure victims checking into homeless shelters. The writer described West driving around with the plants, her hats, and her flowered dresses on the night she was ousted from her house.

I remembered the article and wanted to know how she was doing. Better. Four years after checking into a homeless shelter, West is now living in Euclid, in a rent-subsidized apartment complex surrounded by industrial parks. The shrubbery is a little scraggly, but pink roses bloom. Bright gold door knockers punctuate the quiet hallways.

After that first night in her car, West spent nine months bouncing from acquaintance to acquaintance. It was easier to ask an outsider for a place to stay, she says, than someone in her family.

"Everybody's out there hurting for money," West says of her family, including her three grown children. "You can't just go to somebody and say, 'can I borrow something?' They don't have it either."

She was careful to limit each stay to around three months. "My mother always told me, 'Don't wear out your welcome,'" says West. "Because people, they will say yes but they really don't want to. They're just trying to be nice, to help you out for a while."

After two such moves, she stayed with an upbeat woman she knew only a little through a business networking group. Thankfully, they hit it off. During the time she camped out there, they brainstormed a lot. West was able to sign up for food stamps and map a plan for her life. But then she heard the clock ticking again. "I started thinking, 'You know, I can't stay with her forever. I have to put my pride aside and go to a shelter.'"

Nine months on other people's couches helped her warm up to the idea of shelter living. It also gave her time to go shelter shopping. She used her wits, carefully sizing up all her options because she knew that the wrong choice could send her spiraling. "I went to this one place, and they said, 'We don't have enough beds; you can sleep on the floor,'" she recalls. "I said, 'No, I'm not sleeping on my floor, I'd rather sleep in my car.'" Another shelter wouldn't let her stay there if she had a job, because "they wanted you to be in their program." She set a goal for herself: Get into the women and children's shelter at the West Side Catholic Center in Cleveland's Ohio City neighborhood. "They let you have a job, they help you with your down payment when you find a place, and they also help you with your rent until you get on your feet," West enthuses. "They have a place across the street where you can get clothes."

If you're not a good housekeeper, they have a caseworker train you to keep house, she adds (though she's a good housekeeper). They'll give you pots and pans for your new home and a turkey on Thanksgiving and Christmas.

But the shelter was booked. The person who answered the phone told her to call back every day to see if a spot opened up.

"I did exactly what she said," West recalls. "They got used to who I was. I would call and they would say, 'Hey Miss West, how you doing? No, we don't have an opening. Keep calling.' So that's what I did."

After two months of calling ("I didn't miss a day," she declares), she got in. "That was one of the best decisions I made." She was able to extend her stay at the shelter for a month or two beyond the 90-day limit, then found an apartment. WSCC helped her make rent for a year while she worked part-time.

Today, West is still working as a caregiver and dreams about starting her own business. And maybe someday she'll buy another house. "There's a program right now in Euclid," she says. "You can get a house for $5,000. And they will assist you in getting a $10,000 loan [for repairs]. Once you fix the house up, they will give you the deed, so the house is yours free and clear. I'm thinking about doing that."

Sometimes, when her bedroom gets too hot in summer, she'll come into the living room where it's cooler and sleep by her plants.

"I'm happy now," she says. "It was a learning experience for me. I had to go through that. I'm in a different place now. I like it. I really like it."

§

Kirsten Rosebrock-Hayes and her husband, Tom Hayes, are on paper a world away from West, who took a few courses at a community college and worked in service jobs before she started running her own group home. Kirsten and Tom have four masters' degrees between them and professional jobs as librarians. West is black, her children are grown; Kirsten and Tom, who are white, have two small children. West couldn't rely on her family and had no savings; Kirsten and Tom enjoyed the benefits of both.

Kirsten didn't panic in 2011 when Tom got laid off from his job as a head librarian at Case. She also stayed comparatively calm that December, when they stopped paying their mortgage, and the following August, when, after falling way behind on their credit-card payments, they decided to declare bankruptcy.

"I told my husband, 'I feel like I'm at the top of a high dive and I don't want to jump in,'" she recalls of signing the bankruptcy papers. "And he said, 'You just have to jump.'"

It wasn't until last May, when the bank finally came to take their 1800-square-foot home in Cleveland Heights, that Kirsten got scared. The couple has two kids in elementary school, and they weren't sure where they were going to lay their heads at night.

"I was such a Pollyanna about everything," she recalls. "From the minute my husband got laid off, I thought 'everything's going to be fine; things are going to be great.' And finally this spring, right towards the end of school, I really started to break down: 'I don't know what's going to happen!' Because at that point we did not have anywhere to live, but we had to get out."

The couple's troubles begin as far back as 2003, when they refinanced their home on East Overlook. They had paid $129,000 for it in 2000. They took out a $30,000 home equity line of credit, and used the money to make repairs and pay off some credit card debt they'd racked up.

"Tom always said that was our first mistake," says Kirsten. "We used our credit cards all the time back then. And really didn't pay off the monthly balances." They refinanced again in 2004 with $30,000 in credit card debt, right before the housing bubble burst; at the time, their home was appraised at $240,000.

When Tom lost his job, they owed $202,000 on a home that was worth $130,000 on a good day. Their house payments had ballooned from $1,000 to $1,800 a month. They couldn't make their payments and they were under water, so they chose foreclosure.

But the family didn't have to sleep in their car or entertain the idea of doing shelter drive-bys. When they got the notice from the county about the sheriff's auction of their home, they were already in the market for a new one. They cashed in Tom's $120,000 401K from his job at Case, which after taxes left them with about $100,000 to buy another place.

When the bank came calling in May, Kirsten and Tom had put in an offer on another home in Cleveland Heights. Similar in age and size to their other home, it was a foreclosure that originally had been listed for $180,000, but the price had dropped considerably. Still, there were a few tense weeks of haggling with the realtor who was angling for a better offer than their $78,200. But it all worked out. They got the keys on June 6, three days before the date the bank told them they had to be out of their foreclosed home.

Even with Tom's 401K, they had to do some financial maneuvering to get into the house. Cleveland Heights now requires that homebuyers put money in escrow to repair violations on their new homes,

Kirsten says. The house needed a new roof and plumbing and electrical fixes that would cost an estimated $8,500. All told, they needed double that amount—half for the escrow, and half to pay the repair crews so they could get their escrow money back.

Tom was still out of work, but Kirsten, who'd worked part-time since 2005, had taken a full-time job as the Upper School librarian at Laurel, a private girls' school. Their bankruptcy still fresh, they couldn't get a loan. Instead, Tom's parents agreed to take out a loan and lend them $20,000 with the agreement that Tom and Kirsten would pay them back.

With three days to move, they just started "packing like crazy," says Kirsten. "We did not do a lot of purging. We didn't have time to go through our stuff. So we're doing that more on this end."

When I visited them in August, a repair crew's ladder blocked the front door and the family's belongings were crammed onto every available surface; they hadn't had much time to put things away from the move. As I sat on one of their broken-in couches, I wondered how they had gotten into so much trouble. Their possessions weren't extravagant. In addition to Tom's job loss, Kristen figures it all started by paying for everything with credit cards and then not paying the balance every month. And after her daughter was born in 2005, she switched from full-time to part-time work, so they lost some of their income.

"We really don't have anything. We've thought, 'Oh my gosh, you could take everything in our house and sell it at a garage sale for a couple thousand dollars. Maybe.' We don't go on crazy vacations. I don't buy designer purses."

I marveled at how they managed to buy a house with a fresh bankruptcy and foreclosure on their credit record. "It's pretty impressive," says Kristen. "We have the title to this house. It's really weird. Most people, you've been in the house like 30 years and you have a party because you finally have the title. We *own* this house. But good luck getting a loan."

§

David Rothstein, director of resource development and public affairs for Neighborhood Housing Services, is the co-author of *Broken Homes, Broken Dreams,* a study with the Poverty Center at Case Western Reserve University that looked at 29 families' experiences with foreclosure.

Only a few of those families had reached the point where they actually lost their homes. But the researchers' interviews with them suggested that they had "achieved a greater sense of stability" than families still in foreclosure Siberia. "Having moved out of their homes," the families who lost homes "were moving on with their lives."

But it was hard to know the whole story, because the researchers just couldn't track down many families who'd actually lost their homes. They had "disappeared from the reach of service providers," the study said. "Gaining a more complete understanding of the experiences of these families … is critical to realizing the full impact of foreclosure. How can policy and programs be shaped to increase the possibility of 'success' for these families?"

Rothstein says no one tracks what happens to people after they lose their homes to foreclosure. "This is a real unfortunate thing," he says. "When we started this research project with the Poverty Center, we had a problem because there's no central database for that."

The lack of follow-up troubles him. "These are people who are part of our community," Rothstein says. "Their housing and their lives are as important as anyone else's, and oftentimes their needs are things we can correct."

Cities also need to track these people, to plan accordingly, says Rothstein.

"We need to know if people are becoming renters," he says. "That matters a lot for rental housing, when you can make sure you have enough safe and appropriate-price rental housing if that's where they end up going. If they end up with their parents, that's important for us to know, too. One of the things we started picking up on with this study, are the financial strains [foreclosure] puts on extended families."

Rothstein actually tracked down a third source for me: an NHS client in Bay Village who had been idling in foreclosure for five years after she lost her job as an operating engineer and got two payments behind on her mortgage. But she didn't fit my description, not having lost her home.

"It's a hard thing to find someone who's gone completely through foreclosure," he said. "You're missing the pivotal information that one would have if they had a house: their phone number or an address or an email. That makes it challenging." He adds that if NHS hasn't been able to help a client keep their house—their success rate is 53 percent—that client probably wouldn't answer NHS's request to talk about the experience anyway.

Rothstein hopes that a new NHS program, the Greater Cleveland Stability Project, will better link foreclosure victims, before and after they've lost their homes, to agencies that provide things like food, unemployment and rental assistance. Clients will also receive more help with budgeting and assessing their finances.

"In doing our research study, it occurred to us as we were talking to people, that there's a lot of programs that are supportive of economically fragile families," says Rothstein. "But a lot of people going through foreclosure, they've never entered that type of situation, so they don't know those resources are there or they feel embarrassed or they don't know how to navigate them."

§

Perhaps it's better to have just two stories. Sheri and Kirsten have more in common than you might think. Both lost their homes. And both hustled to lift themselves out of a tragic situation. Sheri's resources were her own persistence, a knack for sizing up helpful strangers, a willingness to ask people for things, and the maturity to wait for the right opportunity. Kirsten's resources were money, education, and family. Even when their finances were a mess and their credit in the basement, both women showed pluck and tenacity, staying up nights figuring out their next move. They make me think about that quote from journalist Alex Kotlowitz, who said he wanted to cover the foreclosure crisis in Cleveland because the people in Cleveland push back.

Both women seem optimistic about the future. Sheri looks forward to the day when she can own her own business. And Kirsten talks about being able to take out a loan in three years for improvements on her new home. But I'm still left wondering: did we learn anything from this crisis? Collective memory fades if the victims have moved out of town, or are essentially voiceless because they've been knocked down a few notches on the class scale. If we don't continue to follow these stories after the bank comes in and the vacate stickers go up, I fear we won't learn a thing.

Dispatches from the Rust Belt

VI. First Person

Is this CLE?

Eric Anderson

Moundsville

David Faulk

T*here is a story that has circulated my hometown* like an intractable conspiracy theory for as long as I can remember. In the nineteenth century, so the story goes, the town elders were given a choice between hosting West Virginia's state penitentiary, or a soon-to-be-announced land grant university. These practical men, given the choice between free prison labor and a standing army of fuzzy-minded professors, leapt at the former. One is tempted to throw in a "the rest is history" here, but such historical determinism has its faults. There have since been too many possibilities at redemption for that choice to have dictated a destiny. And besides, the narrative is awfully clean cut, suspiciously so, even for that historical cliché. No, what makes the story so compelling is not its explanatory simplicity, or even whether it passes the smell test of truth, but rather that choosing a prison over a university is just the sort of thing that people where I come from *would* do.

Moundsville, West Virginia, lies on the east bank of the Ohio River, just a short barge and tugboat ride downstream from Pittsburgh. We drink the Steel City's waste water and brownfield runoff, in fact. This forgotten outpost of boarded-up smelters and steel mills lies just beyond the Pittsburgh Metropolitan Statistical Area per "the Feds," as we liked to call them while playing Cowboys and Indians. Even at a tender age, we usually identified with the Indians. It does not matter much to us where we technically belong. Reality prevails here. Of the variety of industrial manufacturers that once lined the river before the economic apocalypse of the early 1980s, all that remain are the anus end of some coal mines, paint plants and a few chemical manufacturers, which yield products similar to those which caused a disaster in Bhopal, India.

To be working-class in Moundsville was to be truly on the bottom of the slag heap of society. Shunned by Pittsburghers and Clevelanders for its southerness, and by the rest of West Virginia for its sundry north-of-the-Mason-Dixon Catholicisms (mostly Italians and Eastern Europeans, with an occasional Greek thrown in), the northern panhandle of West Virginia can even shun itself. This was most recently witnessed when country music star and favorite son of Glen Dale (just north of Moundsville) Brad Paisley went on Jay Leno to defend his song "Accidental Racist," which is about how it has become unacceptable to wear a Confederate flag t-shirt. For the record, West Virginia entered the Union as a free state in 1863 and fought on the blue side. But most locals don't know that. Whenever this neurotic northern sliver of West Virginia is missing from CNN's crude election-night maps, moral outrage follows. Residents are flummoxed by assertions that this place does not in fact exist.

My ancestors were Asturian Spanish, stocky little human espresso machines who came to West Virginia from the silver mining regions of the old country during the 1920s. Their expertise in mining and smelting was in great demand. They lived in Spanish Row's squat matchbox-like houses, in a little bastion of Papism and domestic violence located down the street from the constant clink-hum of the Pepsi bottling plant. The matchbox simile is not imprecise. Inside these matchbox houses were little hot-headed match people who threatened to explode with self-destructive violence if rubbed the wrong way.

Pepsi was the official non-alcoholic drink of Spanish Row, the bottling plant having been owned by one of its enterprising residents. The Asturians in my family shrub were too proud to sign anti-anarchist and communist statements at Ellis Island, and subsequently redirected to Cuba to mellow out a bit. They made it through Ellis Island in a more amenable state of mind a few babies later. Lured by posters offering mining work in West Virginia, they wound their way through the Alleghenies and northern Appalachians, carrying their stubborn erect postures into the heart of darkness. Photos show them in tight cruel shoes and starched collars, staring uncomfortably into the flash of the camera.

They were known to abuse cats.

The *Asturianos*, too proud to refer to themselves as Spaniards, did not take well to the local customs, I am told, or rather the locals did not take well to them. Holed up at the windowless Peso Club down the street from Spanish Row, the *Asturianos* organized labor after being fired as prison guards for agitation. It was at the Peso that I had my first Pepsi out of a frosty mug pulled from a horizontal deep-freezer by a thin guy attired in an impeccable white undershirt. The Peso was cold, winter cold, like the frosty mug, the coldest place I had ever been during the summer. The *Asturianos* back in Spain, the stay-at-home Monteses and Zapicos, became legendary anti-fascist fighters in the 1930s. Some lived on in exile in Paris as late as the 1990s. I tell their story knowing I am attempting to make identity lemonade out of identity lemons.

From the employment of my grandfather to my junior high school education, the penal colony on Jefferson Avenue, the State Pen, played a greater role in my life than anyone will ever know. My junior high school was overrun by the progeny of inmates from all over the state seeking proximity to dad's weekend visitation. These violent miscreants, challenged in basic hygiene, were promptly labeled "dirt balls" and considered genetically predisposed to all sorts of degenerate acts in the restrooms and locker rooms. They played a central role in our needy psyche: They were people we could look down on.

§

When I first heard the term "Rust Belt" during my last year of junior high, the rust had barely formed on Moundsville. I immediately assumed this was a reference to the local repurposing of a fashion accessory as a disciplinary device, a tactic that increased in response to the stresses of rapid deindustrialization. Childhood infractions small and large were reacted to all the same. The belt was released by grimy mill hands, swung with cracking precision, and re-sheathed between frayed belt loops, all in a matter of seconds. The Ohio Valley in the early 1980s was marked by patterns: For every mill closure, bankers closed in on the houses. Women dried their eyes with pink Kleenexes, and the belts came off. Then families moved away or fell apart.

I have always wondered whether Moundsville suffers under a curse. The mammoth stone-walled penitentiary we called the "butt hut" was ruled unfit for even prisoner habitation. It was repurposed as a federally-funded SWAT team training facility, until it was discovered that the mock explosions were releasing unsafe levels of asbestos. The corrections facility moved to the outskirts of town, in the foothills off a road called Fork Ridge.

Across the street from the abandoned butt hut, the city's namesake, the 69-foot-tall Grave Creek Mound stands like a big green earthen tit. The Adena mound-building civilization populated this region between 1000 and 200 B.C., or "before the curse" as we said in school. Our mound is thought to have been built near the end of this period. Early Moundsvillean, amateur archaeologist, and tomb raider Delf Norona promoted exploratory shafts dug into the mound and exhumed bodies. Thus we speculate a curse not unlike that of Chief Cornstalk's curse in downstream Point Pleasant, West Virginia, which local lore claims as the backstory behind *The Mothman Prophecies*.

There is a distinct possibility that I have personally contributed to Moundsville's curse. Of many nights spent drinking cheap regional beer on the peak of this venerable structure, one evening stands out in particular.

The late summer evening was cool, but tired, with the feel that it was finishing off a muggy day. The chill blew off the river as I met up with Chet and Greg at the shopping plaza. We stood around smoking cigarettes, bored and feeling taller than we were. The idea came to Chet to buy a case of beer, but as none of us had ever drunk any, we weren't sure just how one went about it. Our back was to the drink mart. We talked ourselves into the notion that this purchase should be like any other. We pooled our discretionary income. It came to $8.50, just enough for two six-packs of Rolling Rock and some beef jerky or a case of Iron City Light. We chose the latter. Nobody was hungry.

Chet, an honor student like the rest of us, was a dreamer, unable to focus on anything. His drunken old man railed at him every morning until Chet agreed to pull the lawn mower from the shed in the alleyway and canvass the neighborhood for work. He found plenty. The first half of the summer went by rather uneventfully, until one day Chet was distracted by some flight of fancy and allowed the mower to roll backwards over one foot. With a dull thud and the sound of cracking bone, the mower stalled. A large toe, covered in wet grass clippings, landed on the sidewalk. Without that toe, Chet walked with a slight limp. It didn't seem to bother him.

We made our way past signs for the impressive-sounding Grave Creek Mound Archeological Complex. One of us suggested drinking right there. We turned in unison and looked up at the mound, knowing full well that the only place worth drinking on this property was at the heights. Greg and I hoisted our sacramental offerings over the green chain-link fence to Chet who waited on the other side. We carried the beer up the spiraling stone stairwell to the statue at the mound's peak. The sun was setting behind the Com-Ed coal-fired power plant across the river, rendering the horizontally-blown white smoke in hues of red and orange. Horizontal exhaust meant clear days ahead, the smoke stack serving as a sort of primitive Weather Channel. Two blinking jets on the way to somewhere very different from Moundsville left puffy contrails in the sky. The red sunset bounced off the muddy water below, giving the image of a river on fire.

We plopped down on a stone wall and just stared at each other silently before Chet popped open the first beer. Greg and I followed suit and all three of us grimaced at the taste. The cold Iron City Light stung with an unfamiliar bitterness, something like a blend of tonic water and gasoline.

From the peak of the mound we had a clear view over the penitentiary walls. What I had thought was one gargantuan building in my youth was actually a massive four-story wall, as thick as a car is wide. Inside was a complex of buildings, an open-air hell. It was a mysterious place occupied by murderers and child rapists, eerie long before it was closed down and turned into a place for freak tours and Halloween haunts. Criminal silhouettes danced on frosted window panes.

Stories abounded about the pen. Like the guy who was burned alive by gasoline in his cell during a riot, or the warden with a German name and knee-high leather boots who would challenge prisoners to fights after removing his badge.

Chet turned around and commented on the glow of the sunset. We turned around with him, and then we saw it. A truck jacked up to a ridiculous height bounced down the street, pitching and yawing with each seam in the road surface. Oversized exhaust pipes jutted vertically out of the truck's bed. The driver slouched in the seat, with his right hand low on the steering wheel near his dick and his left arm leaning on the door. His female passenger sat at his side, snuggled close on the bench seat, *a la mode* at that time. As the truck rounded a corner, the driver leaned his head out of the window and released a dark stream of chewing-tobacco juice in a manner only made possible by dental peculiarities.

"High-altitude Hillbilly," Greg blurted out. The spitting driver was no doubt one of the ridge-running locals who found his identity in southern West Virginia, while Chet was the type who looked northward along the industrial riverfront for his. On this mound we straddled the fault line of two cultures.

"A good case for forced sterilization," said Greg ruefully. Greg was back on his forced sterilization soapbox again, a theme he had beaten to death that summer. Greg had thoroughly absorbed—to its dangerous conclusion—the elitist mindset of the gifted program's lead teacher, who flaunted a doctorate in education from the state university that Moundsville passed up.

"Actually, if you want to sterilize people, you could start here," insisted Greg, pointing epiphanically toward the penitentiary, which by now was lit up brighter than a Steelers game on Monday Night Football. A guard was visible in a Gothic-style turret, looking around with binoculars during what must have been a shift change. The guard turned and looked in our direction. I thought about my grandfather, who died decades before my birth, climbing that same guard tower and perusing the grounds with his binoculars. The houses on the hills surrounding the town stared darkly like pillboxes.

"You can't just sterilize people," said Chet. "They are still people."

Chet and Greg's friendship had been strained since The Betrayal, when Greg chose to play on the laughingstock football team rather than play trumpet in the state-champion marching band. It was an unexpected move, given Greg's complete lack of sports experience and his three years in the junior high band. He wasn't athletic, he was just big. He would play defense.

The acrimony between the band and the football team was the most talked-about conflict in the town, after the inevitable union-management conflicts. The band made the team seem like an appendage of a music show. It was safe to say that most spectators turned out to watch the band, and not the football games already given up for lost. The coach and band director were no longer on speaking terms. The band entered the field at the same time as the team, which more than once led to a smashed tuba or broken bass drum. It seemed vaguely revolutionary at the time to see the football team as the side act surrounding the halftime music show. Later in life, when I had a greater appreciation for sports and a suspicion of military-influenced music, I came to see this was an omen that there was something wrong in our universe. Greg took a loud slurp from his beer and sat silently.

"What about Fred?" I asked. Fred was the elderly wash boy at the local Ford dealership. He had done some hard time for chopping up his wife and her lover with an axe. He had caught them in the act while returning home early one day. Fred, one of the few black men in town, became a sensation after his release, treated as a hero and given a $50 a day sinecure at the dealership. He mostly sat leaning against the door-jamb and picked his teeth with a Bic pen.

"Yeah, we can't sterilize Fred," said Chet. Greg had to concede the point. "Besides," added Chet, pointing to the penitentiary, "most of the people in there are in for life. They can't replicate their DNA anyway. You can't knock up a butt." Chet was proud of his use of the word "replicate."

Greg sat silently, unable to find a response. He took another slow slurp at his Iron City before smashing the can and throwing it down the side of the mound.

"Well, I'm just saying that it makes sense in theory," said Greg. "I'll admit that there are problems in practice … like Fred. That has to be sorted out. "

Greg had been reading Herodotus. He had found a dusty copy of the Greek historian's writings in a local library. Greg told us the story of a leader who had been toppled by an enemy force. The leader was forced to watch a procession of his family being marched off to death, but he only cried when he saw one of his servants in the procession. We sat for a while and debated why that could be, concluding that stories are more powerful when they lack clear explanations.

I stood thinking about the earthen protuberance on which we stood, thinking about all that has transpired since this dirt was piled upon bones upon dirt. Rome went on a conquering binge. Christ was crucified. The Jews were driven from Jerusalem. The Sassanid Empire rose in Iran, and Constantinople became the capital of the Eastern Roman Empire. The Vandals sacked Rome and China was reunified under the Sui Dynasty, Muhammad died, Arabs seized Constantinople, Charlemagne was crowned Holy Roman Emperor, the Tale of Genji was written, the Crusades were crusaded and Saladin reconquered Jerusalem. Genghis Khan croaked. The Hundred Years War began and ended in about a hundred years. The Bible was translated into God's language of English, and America was "discovered." Jews were ejected from Spain, Copernicus wrote, and Bruno burned. The Ming Dynasty was formed, and the Gregorian calendar was adopted. Cromwell croaked, America revolted, the French revolted, Karl Marx, the Bolsheviks, 20 million dead in World War II, gas chambers, the atom split, Jews return to Palestine, Beatlemania and the Ayatollah.

And now the civilization on this little speck of earth was falling apart. But the mound would remain. And so would the penitentiary, a testament to Moundsville's true work: locking people up and desecrating the dead. Everything around us was changing except the stars in the sky. Under that postcard-picture sunset stood the fragile, naked life of our drunken bodies.

Lunch Ladies, Lost Cat

Becky Cummings

Cleveland, Ohio
West 10th Street
2007

I *got my two cats when they were little poofs of orange fluff,* rescued by the lunch lady who worked at the isolated New Hampshire boarding school where I was teaching. She pulled them out from under a double-wide trailer not long after they were born.

Now I'm teaching theater at a variety of places in Cleveland. I live in a little bungalow in a walkable neighborhood on the West Side, Tremont. The little orange fur balls are large orange tiger cats with mustard-colored eyes. Their names are short for TOMato and AsparaGUS. T.S. Eliot writes of Gus the Theater Cat, from which I stole the name. Tom and Gus weigh about 14 pounds each.

Gus, the Manx, has long, pointy ears like Spock. He's goofy Garfield orange. His hind legs are bigger than a normal cat's, ramped up like big tires on a monster truck. Manx cats come in three different tail lengths: nubbies, stubbies and shorties. Gus' stubby is a furry pom-pom that moves up and down. He doesn't walk straight but sidewinds like a snake, shoving up against your legs, rowling for attention. Gus is more nervous than Tom.

Tom with the tail is a slightly more sandy color. He purrs in an appealing resonant tone. Like a modern dancer, he gracefully moves his head and shoulders and suddenly curls up on the ground, his stomach exposed, his paws limp in a fey gesture. He charms. He rolls. He is the Cary Grant of the two. Suddenly you find yourself crouching down to pet him. He will twitch his back, roll over, adjust so that you can scratch both sides. He comes up to family and friends and throws himself down in front of them, demanding to be adored.

Tom and Gus are my friends. They hang out with me as I weed the flower beds. Standing regally, blinking at bugs, flicking a tail at flies, digging up worms. They curl up with me at night and become butterbean balls in the crook of my knees as I watch movies. We greet each other when we return home from our travels.

I'm proud that I've kept them alive. I know that doesn't sound good. I'm terrible with house plants, always forgetting to water them and then feeling guilty when they turn to dust and crumble.

Tom and Gus are indoor/outdoor cats. They have a cat door in the window. They jump up onto a red stool outside and push their heads and then bodies through the opening, and ooze out like play dough onto an end table on the inside. Maybe it's like pushing through the birth canal—but with this door, you can go back from where you came.

Then Tom is gone. I don't see him for a day and then two and then three. It's October, getting cold, and the light is waning, the leaves crumbling and cluttering the sidewalk. I call his name. I wander through the backyard, peering over fences and under bushes. Still no Tom. So I begin walking around Tremont, a neighborhood on the Near West Side of the Cuyahoga River in Cleveland. It was a neighborhood that had been there for a long time, many of the old beautiful houses, built by the immigrant workers who had worked in the steel mills in the valley below. Some say the area has the highest number of historic churches per square mile in the country. It sits along the edge of the Cuyahoga Valley. Below, the river snakes under steel bridges reaching across with Xs. You can stand at the edge of the town and look across the river at the downtown landscape. The tall proud buildings, the Terminal Tower, the boats slowly moving up and down, the seagulls calling out loneliness and diving into the wind. Here is something magnificent in the crumble and decay and transformation of brick mortar and steel.

Passing out fliers for the lost cat Tom, I round the corner of

Merrick House, a nonprofit school and community center. There are three kids on a playground

"Hey!" I wave. The kids run to the fence. Green iron gates hold us back from each other, elegant Victorian bars.

"Would you guys let me know if you see my kitty? He's been missing since Tuesday." I pass the flier in through the bars.

"Oh ... he's so cute," says one girl.

The kids look down at the paper, yanking it from one another's hands. They whisper to concur..

The leader kid: "Hey. We've seen your cat."

"Really?"

"The lunch lady at school."

"The lunch lady?"

"On Tuesday, when it was pouring rain? The lunch lady at our school, she looked at this big wet yellow cat. It was just sitting there. So sad. Soaked. She grabbed it. Put it in her car."

"For real?"

"Yes."

My heart beats so fast. I feel adrenaline surge through me.

My bungalow is tucked away behind a large Victorian House. Across the street looms the Tremont Elementary School, a big three-story brick building surrounded by a black iron gate one might picture around some fancy old graveyard. The back of the kitchen opens up on 10th St. A cement ramp slides up to two silver doors. The cafeteria staff would slip out onto the slight slope for a break. Catch a little sunshine or a little smoke and a little gossip and head back in. Near lunchtime, a roar like the sea coast of small voices crashes around the gymnasium walls, a cinderblock two-story hole that doubled as a cafeteria.

I sprint right around the block, cross the street and pound on the silver doors that separate me from my kitty. Big silver nautical boom boom boom. The door opens and a woman with a large nose and a hair net peeks out at me.

"What?"

Another lady pushes out past the first and puts a cigarette to her lips.

"Move over Charlene, I got ten minutes to get my fresh air." She steps to the side and flicks a banana-yellow Bic lighter, lights her cigarette, blows smoke out of the side of her mouth and narrows her eyes at me. She throws her weight against the silver double doors. They clank securely shut.

"We don't buy nothing from people who sell stuff."

"No soliciting."

"Yeah, no solicitors." .

"I need help." I get out my flier. I tell them about my situation, about the kids, about my cat. I gesticulate wildly. "I think Mrs. Shivelly has my cat!"

They step back. They look at my face. Their faces soften. They take my flier.

"Well, she's not here right now. We'll take a flier and give it to her."

She parks right there on the street. They point in front of my house. The woman throws down the end of her cigarette and clamps her white tennis shoe toe to put it out.

The next day, I get up early. I walk around the block to the coffee shop, Civilization, and buy two raspberry croissants and two small coffees. I balance all this on a cardboard carrier and load it up with half and half and sugar, in case Mrs. Shivelly likes those. I wait on the strip of grass between the sidewalk and the road. I look like a butler. I wait for Mrs. Shivelly's red car. I wait and wait and wait. Eventually, she pulls up and parks. A woman in her mid 50s with an auburn ponytail scowls at me. I move toward her with the bag of treats, coffee, and a flier.

"I'm looking for my cat. I heard that you might've picked him up."

"I know. I heard."

"Want some coffee?" She waves away the coffee.

"The cat I got? He ain't your cat."

"Oh." I'm deflated. "You sure?"

"Yeah, I'm sure."

Frowning, she lugs a heavy canvas bag from the back of her car. I lean forward to adjust the front seat lever so it opens up. Her back to me, she stiffens. She turns to face me.

"Look, this guy is skinny, not taken care of. I seen him around for awhile. He's not yours."

"Oh. Okay."

"Sorry. I can't help you."

"Please take this flier in case you might see him."

She slams her car door, beeps it locked, takes the flier and smashes it into her bag. She marches across the street to the school. The big silver doors slam shut behind her. I feel shaky. I sit down stunned on the grass for a moment. The sun is warm. It's a beautiful fall day. Except I lost my cat. I look in at the pastry and they have become a crushed heart failure oozing out of crumbly filo dough. I stand up. I begin to walk. I walk and breathe deep. The leaves are dropping and whirling, scuttling and scuffing.

Ten minutes later, my cell phone whirs away in a desperate ring in my pocket. I put everything down on the sidewalk and finally find the phone. It's Mrs. Shivelly. Her voice is different now, softer, full of tears.

"It's not your cat," she says.

"It's okay."

"He's just skin and bones."

"It's okay," I say again. "Thanks for calling."

"He didn't have a home."

"Well now he has a home," I say.

"I want you to come over and see the cat."

"I don't need to do that."

"I want you to see it isn't your cat."

"It's fine. I really appreciate you calling back."

"I'd feel better if you did."

"Uhm. Okay. When?"

"Now. Meet me back at the car."

I scamper back. Mrs. Shivelly clicks open the car and I open the door. I figure she lives in the neighborhood. We'll go a couple blocks around the corner to see the cat. She drives through Tremont, making a couple turns. Silence. She turns on her signal and we turn right onto a ramp that takes us to 490 East. To our right, the steel mills blow smoke, the rusty smoke stack reproducing the material that made it. To our left, downtown Cleveland's familiar skyline slips by. Seagulls drift on warm drafts over the Flats.

I sit in silence with the two coffees in my lap. One dark, the other cream. I sip from one and then the other.

Mrs. Shively begins to talk.

"After you left, I thought about it."

"Yeah?"

"I want you to see it."

"I believe you."

"I thought, you know what? I'd hate it. If I was you? Thinking that maybe my cat was alive. My cat was alive and living with someone else. Drove me crazy. I couldn't take it."

490 turns into 77 South. I remember, age 10 or 11, riding north up 77 from Richfield to Cleveland with my family. My sister and I dressed up. Colored stockings on. Dresses. We were headed downtown to see The Nutcracker.

As soon as we wheeled around the ramp to East 9th my mom demanding, "Lock your doors! Lock your doors!"

Our locks weren't electric then. We pressed the silver golf tee down with our own pointer finger. Clunk. Click. Safety. Later still, when the silver paint flaked off one revealing plastic, I was like, "Whoa, the world is not what it seems. What would my mom think now?" Thirty years later I sit in a car with a stranger, a lunch lady, going South on 77 to see a cat that isn't mine. The road turns into 480 East and we zip along the two-mile bridge stretching across the Cuyahoga valley. I sit in silence. Waiting. For what I didn't know. And then she begins.

"My husband died." The coffee's now cold.

"Oh. I'm sorry. When?"

"Eleven months ago."

"How?"

"Heart attack."

"What was his name?"

"Jerry. He worked for the steel mills most of his life."

"I'm sorry."

"Yeah. Didn't know I would miss him so much, you know?"

We get off at Garfield Heights. Twenty-five minutes later, 15 miles from the spot where I lost my cat and she picked up another yellow tiger stray, we pull into a neighborhood of '70s split-level ranches.

"Okay." She stops the car and look at the house for a second.

"Is this where you and Jerry lived?"

"Yeah. For 20 years."

"That's a long time."

We enter through the garage. There is a 1970 sky-blue Ford XL convertible with a white top.

"That was my Dad's car. Jerry was working on it. My grandkids want it now. But I just can't."

She leads me down a long hallway and opens the door of a bedroom. There is some scuttling sound and a slinky skinny cat peeks from behind a velour recliner. Orange tiger cat, a teenager, not been neutered and is forming the masculine face of a cat man, peers at us nervously.

"You're right," I say. "That's not my cat."

We turn around and walk back outside and get back in the car,

"I just wanted you to see."

"Thank you."

"I imagined you wondering all the time, you know, wondering and wondering if that was your cat and I didn't want you to do that."

"Thank you."

"You're welcome." She's looking straight ahead. The cityscape is like a small monopoly set on the horizon.

"Did you name him?"

"Yeah. Pooky Bear."

"Like Garfield's teddy bear?"

"Yes. Jerry and I used to really laugh over that comic strip."

"Must be strange to yell 'Pooky! Pooky!' out into the neighborhood."

"Oh. He's not going outside. Pooky stays in."

"Okay."

"Sorry he's not your cat."

"Yeah.

It begins raining, surprising splashes on the windshield. She turns on her wipers, smeary bleary. We're passing the former LTV Steel office building now vacant with a "for rent" sign on top of it. Up ahead in the valley, the flame leaps like a belch out of hell.

"Sorry your husband died."

"Me too."

Mrs. Shivelly slips back into the parking space, as if we never left. I felt like we had traveled far. Father than I ever expected to travel that day. We look at each other. Maybe we smile. We're strangers and yet we've shared what we lost. Maybe that was just what she needed, to tell a stranger on the highways of Cleveland how much she missed her husband who died.

"Well, thanks," I say. I offer the coffee.

"I don't drink coffee," she says. "It makes me shake." I pour it out onto the grass, covered in leaves.

"But I will take the pastry."

"Cherry strudel," I say. "It's smooshed."

"Thanks," she says. And takes the bag. We say goodbye. She walks across the street and joins the other two lumpy lunch ladies outside. They're smoking. After a second, they all turn to look at me and I wave, they wave.

Maybe it's because I'm not looking, but I don't see that lunch lady again.

§

That evening, I got a call from a woman whose backyard is backed up to our backyard, separated by bushes and shrubs.

"I think your cat is in our barn."

"Oh gosh!"

"I drove up tonight and there was a little cat face looking out of the top window. My little girl says we don't have a cat. Then we found your flier in the mail."

"I can't believe it."

"We cleaned the barn this weekend. We must have shut him in."

I run around the block with the cage in hand. Their home is a beautiful urban rehab of an old farmhouse. Pumpkins carved with lopsided grins sit on steps. Corn stalks tied to porch posts. Rust-colored mums welcome fall. I knock on the door and am greeted by a woman with honey-blond hair. Two kids peek from either side of her. I'm anxious, but stop to smile at them and their shyness. The little girl points to the barn in the dark out back.

"He's in there," says the mom. "My husband will help you out."

A tall man wearing an old faded red cotton baseball hat and a navy polyester vest from Eddie Bauer smiles at me and motions me to follow. I take the cage and we go back towards the dark barn. He shoves opens the door with a creak and a crack. The door slides aside on hinges, creating a wide-open grin into darkness. No lights in the barn. I charge in with only the dim glow of street and porch lights to help me navigate around boxes and tools.

"Tom!" I call. "Tom, Tom!"

His response. A loud forlorn howl. It's him!

"Oh, Tom!" I yell.

"Meowrh!!" I clamber halfway up the stairs to the loft and Tom slinks down, body pressed to the floor. I grab hold of him tight. He's dusty and a bit ratty and skinny, but he's my Tom. I press him to me awkwardly and gangly kissing his boney head. I shove him into the cage which the man is holding and together we bring the cage outside.

I look at the man and he is looking at me with wide eyes of concern.

"Oh my god!" I say. "Thank you thank you thank you!" I throw my arms around the stranger and begin to cry. I sob, I weep, I laugh, I sob some more.

I thought he was gone. I thought I'd never see him again. I thought it was my fault. I thought he was dead! My emotional dam breaks. Feeling alone, looking for things we lost, wandering through the neighborhood, not recognizing the world. Sometimes we fear that will we will never see people again and sometimes we don't. Sometimes people leave and cats get lost and they don't come back. And it is almost unbelievable that strangers step in and hold you for a minute, while you lose your balance. Eddie Bauer man and me, two strangers hugging and swaying on a cement driveway, under the basketball headboard, in between parked cars. Tom in the cage, grumpy and looking up at me, his little fuzzy face, my friend returned.

I pull myself together, pick up the cage and we move back into the light. The kids want to peek at the cat that lived for days in their barn and isn't theirs. I thank the woman again for calling. The husband comes and joins his family. He puts his her arm around his wife. The two kids stand on either side of their parents. There they stand, all together, all connected, having helped a neighbor reunite a family of another sort. They shake my hand. They say no problem. Then I realize by the tone of the voice of kind Eddie Bauer man that he is deaf. He says "I'm sorry that I didn't catch much of what you said back there in the barn. The light's burned out. I couldn't see your lips. I only read lips."

I pick Tom up in his cage and walk him down the driveway, onto the sidewalk out into the darkness. I turn and look back. They're watching us. I wave. They wave. I turn around and I leave that family there. I've done this before. Leaving. Walking away. Soon we are gone.

§

The calls continue. People are so kind. Tom is home and he is out in the neighborhood again, doing his rounds. People call and say, "He's sitting right here! Right in my yard! Tom your cat!" I go and take down the fliers I can find.

I get one more call.

A husky smoky voice, Marge Simpson as a tenor.

"I got. Yahour cat."

"Oh wow! I found my cat."

"Come and get him."

"I got my cat back."

"What? This isn't your cat?"

"No."

"Whose cat is it?"

"I don't know."

"He's sitting here in my bar eating ham off a paper plate."

"Wow. You treat cats well."

"I treat everyone well. If they deserve it. Hang on. [In the background.] Get down cat! Ya don't own the place."

"I really appreciate your call."

"Ya know who this is?"

"No."

"Ma. Ma Hotz."

"Hello, Ma Hotz"

"I own the bar on the corner."

"I've never been there."

"Ya know what day it is?

"No."

"My birthday."

"Wow! Happy Birthday."

"I'm 87. Don't tell no one."

"Congratulations."

"I want ya to come to my birthday party tonight."

"Tonight?"

"8 o'clock."

"All right. I'll see you then."

"Now I'm gonna let this cat that isn't yours outta here. Come here, cat. Scram cat."

It's cold, the earth has turned away from the sun. I step out into the dark city night. It's the end of October, Halloween and my birthday, too. I breathe in deep the cold air of the end of harvest season. This is my season. This is when I came into the world, in the midst of burgeoning darkness. The sidewalks are old, big slabs of stone, crooked at slants pushed up by thick tree roots. They are like graveyard headstones pitching in a frozen landscape of zombie wonderland. No path on this earth goes smoothly and to expect otherwise is a recipe for disaster. The oak trees forever holding onto their leaves, have sprinkled a few crisps on sidewalks. I step on them, pretending they are giant bug shells.

Up ahead a pink neon sign heats up just a slice of the neighborhood. The corner bar. Hotz Cafe. Ma Hotz, a stranger, invites me into her life. Just for a moment. When you think about it. That's all we've got. The moment. Remember some moments create meaning—there's your life. Without loss, without the search—for my cat, for myself—none of these moments would've happened. I walk towards the Hotz Cafe where life, in one form or another, continues.

Irreverent Passion and a Rooted Ethos

Peter Debelak

*I**t is hard not to notice the resurgence* of Cleveland pride, whether it's proudly worn "216" t-shirts or the seemingly national embrace of "Rust Belt Chic." There are shoots of change occurring in town that give good cause for optimism and pride in our rich history as a legacy city. Downtown is drawing back businesses and residents. Bright spots of tech start-ups and venture capital are attracting attention. A makers' movement is beginning to spill out of previously abandoned industrial buildings and warehouses. Manufacturing, of all things, is a growth industry for the region. Many, like myself, are moving back from escapades on the coasts to raise families, to start businesses, and to re-embrace what embarrassed us at 18.

Despite much cause for optimism, there is a darker undercurrent that still remains firmly in our consciousness as Clevelanders. There remains a sense that we are stuck. That a majority in our region, the people and the institutions, are a bit parochial and resistant to real change. Recent studies have set forth empirical evidence of what we all already suspected: Cleveland lacks an *influx* of ideas and a global connectivity which mark most growing modern metropolitan areas. Our problem isn't "brain-drain," but rather a lack of an influx of migration, ideas, and global connectivity.

There is something about the Rust Belt authenticity which isn't chic at all—it is stuck and resistant to change. It is insular and its communities balkanized.

There is a sense, then, in which "Rust Belt Chic" is at odds with the need for an influx of ideas and change brought by migratory churn and global connectivity.

Yet, this tension is really not problematic at all. In fact, it is inside this tension that lasting authentic change and growth can come to Cleveland. What sometimes manifests as being insular or resistant to change is, at root, a positive and deeply rooted ethos.

The ethos is something difficult to define, but which Clevelanders know intuitively. It is that deep sense that the things we build are a result of hard work and long-term struggle. The things we make with our hands, the objects produced by the harsh monotony of the factory—even our communities, forged through struggle over decades—are the products of our building. And we build things to *last*.

Yet, for many boomerangers or progressive young(ish) people I know in Cleveland (myself included), the culture of Cleveland's insularity and resistance to change can be quite frustrating. The upcoming generation of Clevelanders cares little about the traditions of yore. Recently, an exuberant Pittsburgh blogger captured the enthusiasm and spirit well:

"[I]n the next ten years Pittsburgh's going to be resettled by a wave of people in their 20s and 30s who will not wait for change. They will not nod their heads at cozy backroom deals over stadiums or rail terminals or other publicly traded lands. They won't listen to billionaires breaking the law who talk about "takings." They won't let their neighborhoods be shoved aside by lazy development or substandard schooling or indifferent local government. They will be the government."

There is something absolutely refreshing in this passionate irreverence. This is how to bring new ideas and an influx of migration and global connectivity.

I have lived this passionate irreverence. Fighting for low-income housing in Chicago; suing cities for sweetheart deals to private developers using taxpayer land or money; fighting for community benefits agreements even while promoting such developments; fighting alongside low-income workers to keep hospitals open in low-income neighborhoods; fighting voter-ID laws targeted at low-income communities.

Yet, for me, there is something off-putting about this irreverence, too—even as I place myself in the same category. There is little check on this kind of "big idea"-change to keep Cleveland authentic. For these change-makers, "Rust Belt Chic" is little more than a garment to wear, or a smoke-stack in the skyline. Precisely *because* this group is often more globally connected and has gotten a taste of Austin, Portland, and Brooklyn, their "big ideas" threaten—one unintended consequence built upon the last—a mindless march toward our loss of identity.

It might seem easier, more natural, to bring big ideas into the menial or parochial to inform them in some way. It may make it feel more noble or part of a larger whole. But I find it much more meaningful, now, to bring the daily slog of hands-on work into theoretical thought. I am finding the intuitive thought derived from daily monotony, with introspection, to be razor sharp in cutting away the fat of theory. The seemingly banal forces an attention to human detail and valuable human history that a well-intentioned "big idea" fails to engender.

These days, my passionate irreverence takes a different hue: working with my hands to produce furniture; opening up a workshop to the community and other aspiring makers to enable their own endeavors; working toward internships for low-income kids to learn a craft; joining my fellows to help make Cleveland's independent furniture-making scene a growth industry. These are things that have remarkable possibilities, but will be built slowly over time.

"Rust Belt Chic"—seen not as a loose-fitting garment, but as an *ethos* of hard work and methodical building of something that lasts, benefiting the greatest to the least among us—is a powerful counter-balance to "bring Silicon Valley to Cleveland!" Let alone the habits of consumption that would follow.

Our goals must not be "change at all costs!" Rather, the manner in how we change matters. The distributive benefits of our change matters. It is an aspirational pragmatism. Big ideas for change, rooted in a substantive ethos of how lasting change happens.

I will reject the "we need an influx of ideas and migrants" narrative if it means we become Portland, unmindful of the value of how our rich history and ethos can inform that change. And I will also reject the "Rust Belt Chic" narrative if it means we glorify our roots and neighborhoods without an open ear to the different-looking neighbor who moves in or ignore the migrant challenge to our parochial ways of being and managing.

Can we live in the tension between a desperately needed irreverence and the subtlety of our rooted ethos? If so, how? I look forward to the unfolding answer.

Dispatches from the Rust Belt

Contributors

Anne Trubek is the founder, editor-in-chief and publisher of Belt.

Erick Trickey is a senior editor at *Cleveland Magazine*.

Jacqueline Marino writes about the interesting people, places and culture of the Rust Belt. She is the author of *White Coats: Three Journeys through an American Medical School* and the co-editor of *Car Bombs to Cookie Tables: the Youngstown Anthology* which will be published in 2015. She is an associate professor of journalism at Kent State University.

Zoe Gould is a writer and educator living in the great city of Philadelphia.

Laura Putre is a senior writer at Belt.

Pete Beatty writes and edits in Cleveland.

Jake Austen is editor of *Roctober* magazine, author of several books, and has freelanced for publications including *Harper's*, *Vice*, *Chicago Tribune*, and *Chicago Reader*. *Playground (Gliteratti Incorporated, 3/14)*, his forthcoming collaboration with Paul Zone, is a coffee table book of photographs and stories from New York's early 70s pre-punk scene.

Daniel Goldmark is Associate Professor of Music at Case Western Reserve University.

Amanda Shaffer is a professional career coach living in Cleveland Heights where she writes about politics, parenting and other irritations at Amandatoryrant.com

G. M. Donley is a Cleveland Heights-based writer, photographer and designer.

A native of Lansing, Michigan, **Edward McClelland** is the author of *Nothin' but Blue Skies: The Heyday, Hard Times and Hopes of America's Industrial Heartland.*

Gordon Young is the creator of Flint Expatriates: A blog for the long-lost residents of the Vehicle City and the author of *Teardown: Memoir of a Vanishing City*, named a Michigan Notable Book for 2014.

Ben Schulman is the Communications Director for the American Institute of Architects Chicago (AIA Chicago) and the co-creator of the Contraphonic Sound Series, a project that documents cities through sound.

Daniel J. McGraw is a senior writer at Belt.

Brad Ricca is the author of *Super Boys*, named a Top 10 Book on the Arts by Booklist and now available in paperback. He is the recipient of a 2014 Cleveland Arts Prize for Emerging Artist in Literature and is a SAGES Fellow at Case Western Reserve University.

Eric Anderson once changed a tire in the Flats while being watched by a pack of wild dogs. Another time, his car broke down on a lift bridge and had to be pushed to the end so an ore boat could pass through. His book of poems, "The Parable of the Room Spinning" is available from Katywompus Press. "Is This CLE?" is available as a limited edition print by contacting the artist at ericanderson@oh.rr.com.

David Faulk is a graduate student in Columbus, Ohio.

Becky Cummings is a writer, teacher, and theater artist in Cleveland.

Peter Debelak is a Cleveland-based furniture maker and co-founder of Soulcraft Woodshop and Soulcraft Furniture Gallery.

About
Belt Magazine

"[Belt] practices principles that ring almost quaint in the new media age ...The result is a selection of stories and essays that often offer fresh insight into regional issues and challenges and that stoke smart conversation." — Robert L. Smith, *The Plain Dealer*

"Creator Anne Trubek has taken the loose idea of writing about the Rust Belt and expanded the catch-all category with a host of brilliant writers on any and all topics that affect us, be it United pulling its hub from Hopkins and what role Burke Lakefront Airport plays in the region, to moving essays on what it's like to grow up, live and work in Cleveland. It's the sort of writing you won't find anywhere else, both in scope and talent." — *Cleveland Scene*

"The decaying cities of the post-industrial Midwest can sometimes seem like a museum of things America used to make: cars, refrigerators, steel, televisions. But if a start-up in Cleveland gets its way, the region may help rebuild the market for another endangered product—long-form magazine journalism." — Jennifer Schuessler, *New York Times*

About
Rust Belt Chic:
A Cleveland Anthology

"[Trubek] and Piiparinen were keen to assemble a Cleveland snapshot that felt more authentic to them: No mindless boosterism or 'ruins porn,' that artistic fetish for fallen-down manufacturing towns. 'Rust Belt Chic' reads like a rebuttal to Richard Florida's argument for Creative Class cool filling cities with young elites." — Karen R. Long, *Cleveland Plain Dealer*

"Instead of sitting back and reading what the national media has to say, local writers Anne Trubek and Richey Piiparinen decided to take hold of this 'rust belt revival' narrative and allow Clevelanders the chance to define what's happening in our city. To, as Trubek says, 'tell it our (Cleveland's) way, from the inside-out, instead of having others describe us to ourselves.' "— Sarah Valek, *Cool Cleveland*

"Rust Belt Chic" illustrates in bold fashion that strength of character abounds in the Cleveland community. That's fitting because inside the pages of the book, that very same audacity of spirit is expressed in literal form." — Freshwater Cleveland

About
A Detroit Anthology

"A Detroit Anthology is one of the surprise hits of the year. While many books have been written on and about Detroit by writers who have visited, this anthology of prose, poetry, and essays is written by the metro area's residents themselves ... it's the wide ethnic array of voices that truly shows the facets of Detroit life. — *Ebony Magazine*

"What Clark has done with these writers is shown that you can have a truly authentic Detroit experience, built from all walks of life. There's city dwellers, suburbanites, new comers to the city (and region), former residents, and people just passing through. In a city that often pits people against each other based on race, class, and geographic location (although this is often linked more closely with the other two factors), [*A Detroit Anthology*] brings everybody to the table to have a voice.
— John Cruz, *The Urbanist Dispatch*

"What these writers share, despite their differences of age, race, gender, and temperament, is the understanding that one has to know Detroit's history before even beginning to imagine how the city might move forward. Rather than trying to explain Detroit, editor Anna Clark says she set out to capture 'the candid conversations Detroiters have with other Detroiters.' She has succeeded spectacularly."
— Bill Morris, *The Daily Beast*

About
The Cincinnati Anthology

"Intent on chronicling the place she's called home since 2011, McQuade went about masterminding *The Cincinnati Anthology*, a deft, well-considered collection of essays, illustrations and photographs that represents, as she writes in her intro to the book, 'the visions of those who have fallen madly in love with the city of Cincinnati, either for the first time or all over again.' " — Jason Gargano, *Cincinnati CityBeat*